MW01166441

MODERN
LUXURY
RESIDENCES

ARTPOWER

Modern Luxury Residences

Copyright © Artpower International Publishing Co., Ltd.

ARTPOWER™

Designer: Wang Anlei
Chief Editor: Li Aihong

Address: Room C, 9/F., Sun House, 181 Des Voeux Road Central,
Hong Kong, China
Tel: 852-31840676
Fax: 852-25432396

Editorial Department
Address: G009, Floor 7th, Yimao Centre, Meiyuan Road, Luohu District,
Shenzhen, China
Tel: 86-755-82913355
Fax: 86-755-82020029

Web: www.artpower.com.cn
E-mail: artpower@artpower.com.cn

ISBN 978-988-19226-2-5

No part of this publication may be reproduced or utilised in any form by any means, electronic or mechanical, including photocopying, recording or by any information storage and retrieval system, without prior written permission of the publisher.

All images in this book have been reproduced with the knowledge and prior consent of the designers and the clients concerned, and every effort has been made to ensure that credits accurately comply with information applied. No responsibility is accepted by producer, publisher, or printer for any infringement of copyright or otherwise arising from the contents of this publication.

Printed in China

PREFACE

True luxury, far from opulence and frivolous ostentation, resides in the emotion that space conveys, in the capacity to personally touch us, with creativity and originality, while remaining pleasant and stimulating in a universal sense.

A luxurious residence incorporates the soul of those who live in it. It is the physical manifestation of their memories, affections and dreams, presented in a unique and inspiring form. It never loses its alluring effect.

A space that integrates with its surroundings and has unforgettable sights of the scenery around it. A construction that respects nature, seeking sustainability and social inclusion. A residence that enables people to respect their own rhythm, allowing for action and creation, or for observation, relaxation and leisure.

A refuge.

A space that harmoniously mixes styles and concepts, from the exclusive to the industrial, from technological to sustainable, from authenticity to everyday life. That cherishes those who live in it, that makes them feel worthy, that shelters, energizes and protects them. A space that suffices the needs of its users in an efficient, but still stimulating way.

A luxurious residence is timeless.

Luxury can have many facets, but in the end, it all comes down to a space that makes us feel as better people.

This book provides many facets of luxury in apartments and houses that compose a diversified scenario, encompassing a great range of identities. An invitation to dive into this diversity that is, by itself, luxurious.

David Guerra Architecture and Interior

⃝ CONTENTS

Project Leader ·
Architect David
Guerra

BELVEDERE APARTMENT

Team / David Guerra, Fernanda Farage, Cori Coraci, Luciana Gontijo   Location / Belo Horizonte, Minas Gerais - Brazil   Total Construction Area / 650 m²   Structure and Service / Construtora Castor   Photography / Jomar Bragança

The project designed by David Guerra Architecture and Interior is located in a noble area of Belo Horizonte, Minas Gerais, Brazil. The apartment is 600 m² and it was inspired in the cosmopolitan style of the inhabitants, a couple without children.

There was no intention to follow to the fad, rather it pursue an elegant and cozy atmosphere using design furniture and works of art.

The bright rooms with a lot of free space and few elements, low and straight furniture, bright wood, white floors and walls as well as transparent curtain increase the space. ●

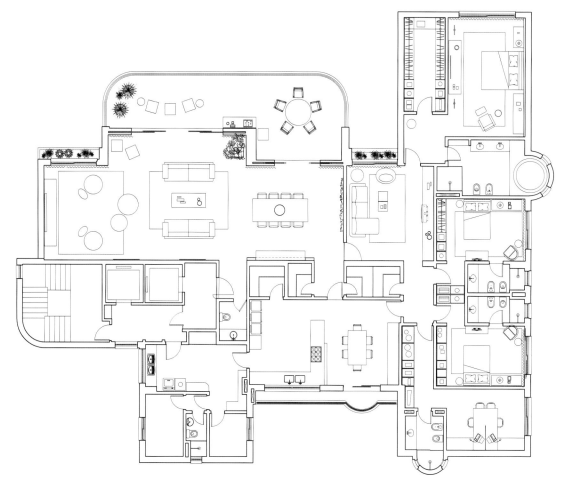

Architect ·
David Guerra
Architecture and
Interior

APARTMENT LA

Project Team / David Guerra, Nínive Resende   Location / Belvedere, Belo Horizonte, Brazil   Photography / Jomar Bragança
Construction Area / 350 m²

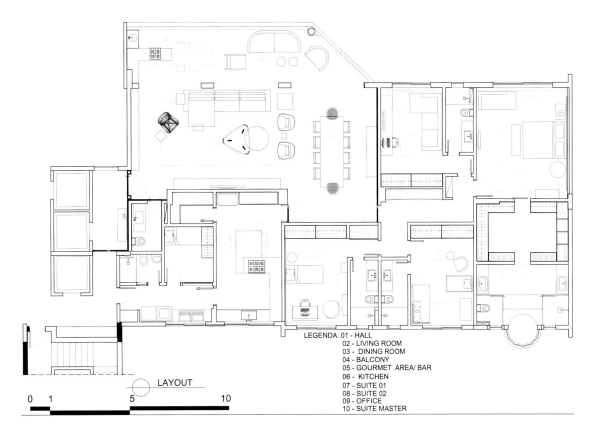

LAYOUT

0 1 5 10

LEGENDA: 01 - HALL
02 - LIVING ROOM
03 - DINING ROOM
04 - BALCONY
05 - GOURMET AREA/ BAR
06 - KITCHEN
07 - SUITE 01
08 - SUITE 02
09 - OFFICE
10 - SUITE MASTER

When their first child started going to school, the couple bought an apartment in the city, leaving the country house, where they formerly lived, as a weekend destination.

The new home combines the cozy aspect of a country house and the urban and practical style of the big city. To attend the needs of the couple with two children, a renovation was needed. The walls that divided the living room from the balcony were demolished, making spaces larger, more fluid and comfortable. The balcony became a gourmet bar/kitchen that can be used for the wine with friends and breakfast in family, with a view to the mountains. Linen sofa and chairs and a vintage armchair create a relaxing living area also in the balcony. A small fireplace has become a major element of the living room wall. The new warming ambience mix colors, rustic and natural materials with modern and technological ones. They are wool, natural linen, nude tones, leather in different colors – honey, whisky and chocolate - wood and demolition wood, gray concrete, Silestone rock, stainless steel, yellow metal, bronze, mirror, glass and acrylic, all materials that combined,

create a great ambience.

The choices of the furniture noted the concern of creating a place that prioritizes comfort, warmth, elegance and relaxation. That way we can see a mix of Brazilian designs, such as from Sergio Rodrigues, Pedro Useche, FredericoCruze, and international designs, like De Padova, Minotti of B&Bitalia, Maxalto, Muuto and Mooi.

In the living area a big sofa with a chaise was reformed by JHJ and gains a new linen covering. Pillows by Entreposto, a Jensen leather armchair from Minotti and an armchair Louisiana from Depadova, prove the pursuit of comfort and elegance. The Sullivan low tables from Minotti (gray glass r ound and wood triangular) along with the Still table, also from Minotti and Lens by Patricia Urquiola add a touch of fun and relaxation to the room. The oak dining table with highlights the beauty, lightness and comfort of the Twombly leather chairs from Minotti and the chandelier by Mooi.

In the gourmet kitchen, a block of graphite Silestone sustains the table of mahogany field, design by the architect; Sérgio Rodrigues chairs indicate the relaxed and comfortable way to receive friends for a dinner or even a drink.

The entire floor of the apartment, except the wet areas, has been replaced by wide planks of mahogany field bought from a farm. The floor has gone through a bleaching process, maintaining the identity and rusticity from the wood and giving a more light and modern touch to the place. On the wall, gray concrete and panels of different types of wood, such as mahogany field, pink mahogany, cedar and cinnamon, bring color and warmth to the room.

The kitchen also provides a mix of materials, the technology of Italian glass Panna and reflective glass, Italian chairs Papiro by B&Bitalia, graphite Silestone on the floor and silver one on the countertops, walls with black and gray hydraulic tiles, wood doors and mahogany table – design by the architect. The kitchen becomes

a mix of personal and contemporary. That mix can also be seen in the toilet, with the gauzy Silestone floor and countertops, burgundy toned concret e, Hansgrohe mixers that contrast with the tile of the wall and the Indian mirror.

In the master bathroom, the priority was the eleg ance, which was achieved by the Limestone Persiano, cabinet with Italian glass and Rimadesio door. In the master bedroom, t he highlights are for the headboard with mahogany with stailess steel profile, Glam lampshade from Pradina, French dresser, linen Selene bed by Maxalto and Pantosh wooden chair. Nude and caramel tones and natural materials, linens, leathers and woods, provide a welcoming place that helps relaxation.

In the boy's room, the colorful and playful fur niture design denotes a hip and timeless style. ●

Project Leader ·
Architect David
Guerra

LOURDES APARTMENT

Team / David Guerra, Gisella Lobato, NíNive Cardoso, Gabriel Barbosa   **Location** / Belo Horizonte, Minas Gerais, Brazil
Total Construction Area / 340 m²   **Photography** / Jomar Bragança

This large apartment, situated in Lourdes, one of the most charming areas of Belo Horizonte, was designed to accommodate a couple with their three young children. The idea was to integrate the spaces and uses.

The living room, in addition to receiving friends with elegance and comfort, is also a place to watch a movie at home, and is integrated with the bar, with a large comfortable carpet and a low coffee table, giving people freedom to stay the way they prefer. The choice of the square table in the dining room allows for conversation during the family meals.

In the TV room, the panel in black lacquer, and the black TV stand, mask the several electronic equipment of the owner, and also create a composition with the old General Electric refrigerator inherited from the owner's grandmother, which was adapted for wine temperature. The black leather sofa and the choice of support tables, instead of a coffee table, give freedom to the children.

The integration of spaces – living room, bar, dining room, TV room and balcony –

brings lightness and fluidity to the space. The decor, with a mix of colors, materials, textures and styles, brings the private universe of the owner, adept of the timeless good things that always remain stylish. There is a great blend of natural linens, leather, different shades of wood, polished marble, rustic granite, steel and acrylic. Various shades of beige, brown, and black create an ambience both modern and cozy, which is enhanced by lighting, and chandelier in the dinner area.

Furniture is both by famous international designers — such as Le Corbusier, Vico Magistretti and Jaime Tresserra — and Brazilian designers — as Sergio Rodrigues, Jorge Zalszupin and Alfo Lisi. Beautiful works of art and objects, with different styles and stories, are displayed around the apartment — such as the Sévres porcelain from the XVIII century; a General Electric refrigerator and sewing machine, both from the owners grandmother; and wooden horse, reminder of the childhood days at the farm. All this helps making this apartment's décor full of personality. ●

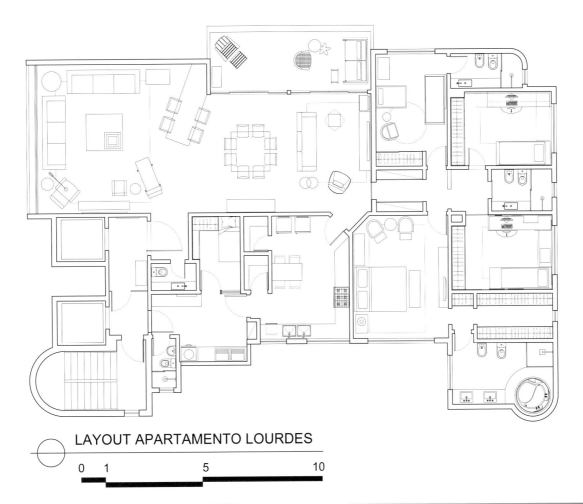

LAYOUT APARTAMENTO LOURDES

0 1   5   10

Architect ·
SHH

CHELSEA APARTMENT

Location / Chelsea, London   Area / 697.00 m²   Photography / James Silverman, Richard Waite

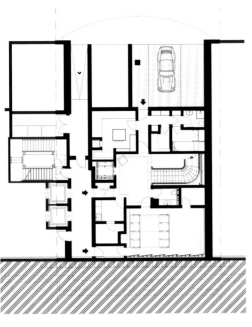

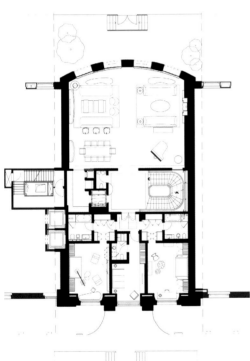

This expansive triplex resides behind the façade of a Victorian 'grande dame' in Chelsea. Purchased as a shell and core of 3 floors, their international client engaged the services of SHH to transform the apartment into a glamorous contemporary haven for him and his family. With hints of Art Deco detailing and a smooth neutral palette, this home blends up-to the minute technology with classical style and opulence. Stand-out spaces include the triple volume entrance space, dominated by a three storey bas relief olive tree. The principal 1,400 sq ft reception room combines a formal and informal entertaining with a dining area, as well as a grand piano. Tucked away behind an automatic mirror door is the family kitchen, whilst beyond the leafy voiles is a private patio which extends to Chelsea's most gorgeous communal garden. The apartment also benefits from 3 further en suite bedrooms, a large cinema with options for watching movies in 3D as well as a Chef's kitchen. ●

Architect ·
Kiko Salomão
Arquitetura

PROJECT 910

Team / Kiko Salomão, Ana Lino, Rafael Palombo, Renata Leite, Giovanna Kuwada, Brunno De Alencar   **Location** / São Paulo , SP Brasil
Area / 515 m²   **Photography** / Alain Brugier

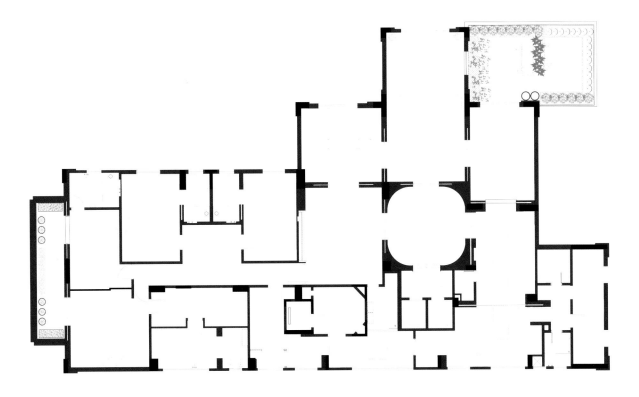

"It cannot be Comercial". That was the first thing said by the young couple that own this apartment when we've had our first meeting and that really get along with our firm's way of working. From that moment on we knew that this work would have strong potencials to be unique.

The original drawing of this flat was completely different and all rooms were quite irregular, with various indentations.

The starting point was the main entrance door. A stainless steel screen, originated from highly modern influences and which, at the end, weighed 1ton.

From the door and throughout all the other details, the project goes by the modern to the contemporary, but always inside the minimalist premisses of our firm.

We were handed the task of proposing a new Project: a gourmet kitchen and another functional kitchen were requested.

The greatest challenge was to locate the gourmet kitchen between the dining room and the functional kitchen of the flat, meanwhile maintaining all areas integrated among themselves.

In addition, the gourmet kitchen occupied a space that is connected to the main gallery of the entry hall, that is, practically at the main entry of this flat.

Some issues were fundamental for the success of this Project: a large counter was proposed along both kitchens, thus unifying them visually. However, we included a glass division over the counter, as well as two automatic glass doors which, when closed, isolate the rooms acoustically, and also keep odours from spreading.

The main colour of the kitchens is a burnt orange reminiscent of the fifties. Thus we believe this would result in a cosy environment not conflicting with the social areas.

This combination between the spaces and its implementation resulted in a perfect solution as visitors arriving at the flat have direct access to the gourmet kitchen.

From the architecture, interior design to furniture design, decoration and art, our firm was focused on creating a precisely detailed, exclusive and timeless project. ●

Design Agency ·
Dariel Studio

THE BLUE PENTHOUSE

Designer / Thomas Dariel   **Designer Assistant /** Justine Frenoux   **Project Manager /** Hata Chen   **Area /** 400 m^2
Photography / Derryck Menere

Crafting a functional yet attractive and unique home for a family is a tall order for any interior designer. Thomas Dariel took up the challenge.

To begin, the designer wanted to break the original basic volumes and open things up more. In the living room, a huge void has been created that gives a very architectural and contemporary feeling while maximizing daylight exposure through large bay windows. The former balcony has also been integrated to the indoor part to increase the sensation of volume and enable more space for leisure. Looking up, a suspended cube has been designed to host the client's office. Consistent with the architectural shapes, wink to the original meaning of the word

penthouse (from the latin appendere – to be suspended), the cube also holds a strong meaning. The client, while working there, is at the same time overlooking his home and his family.

Dariel also wanted to modify the way the spaces r elated to one another. To match this requirement, the staircase has been designed and relocated to be at the center of the apartment. Masterpiece in itself, the staircase is opening, connecting and leading to all rooms. It is the core of the space structure, the heart of the design.

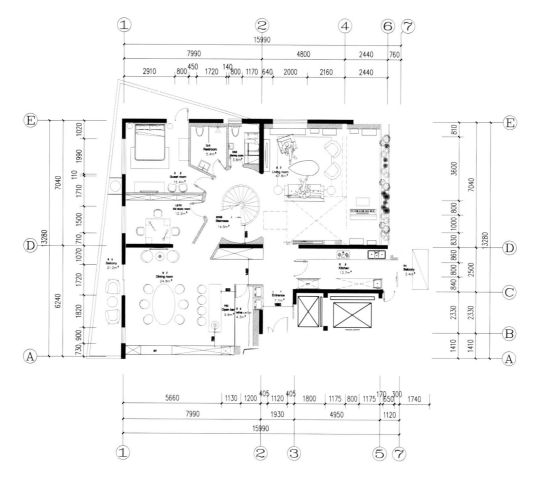

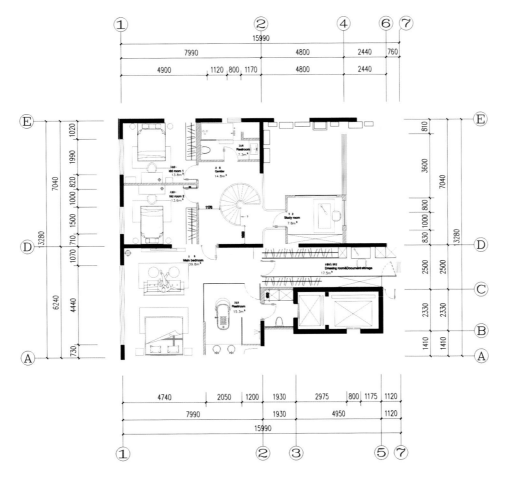

The master plan of the penthouse features traditional functions: kitchen, living room, dining room, bedrooms, study and bathrooms. Yet all have been given specific care to release style, character and identity. The dining room sets the standard of the apartment. While elegant wooden panels in a warm blue-grey tone are covering the entire space, Dariel played with very graphic shapes on ceiling and walls to balance the classical setting with contemporary lines. In the center of the room, the very peculiar geometric B&B dining table, circled by comfortable and rather traditional- looking chairs by Philippe Hurel, answers the same idea. Behind the customized bar counter where the family gathers for breakfast, again a functional yet stylish element, the space features a glass-paneled wine cellar that reflects the living room while allowing a look at the client's wine collection. Inside the cellar, the organic- shaped shelves have been inspired by boats and by the appearance of their hull's wood skeleton.

While the first floor resumes the public functions of the apartment, the second floor accommodates more private and intimate ones. Dariel designed a vitrine-like bathroom, glassed in on two sides. While he aimed to preserve the transparency and the open feeling in the space, the glass partitions are still tinted on the bedroom side. If one taking its bath can have a plain view on the master bedroom, watch TV or further enjoy the skylights behind the windows, one in the bedroom can only guess what is happening in the bathroom. Dariel has also played with the glass-mirror-reflection elements in the dressing room. True art pieces, each doors of this very confidential area have been designed with two layers, one of glass with engraved lines, and below, one of mirror reflecting the glass pattern.

What strokes in the realization of this penthouse is the tremendous amount of details. The space is elaborated and sophisticated, featuring an utterly designed environment where ceilings, walls, storages, furniture have been customized to serve the design purpose. Cabinets, wardrobes and chest drawers, produced by hand, have been inspired by old luggage. As steamer trunks, they are finished with leather and linen and appeal the strong traveling spirit of their owners. In the kids' bedrooms, wallpapers, specifically designed by Dariel Studio's team for the project, bring culture, playfulness and poetry. Throughout the space, AC grills are elegant stainless steel plates with engraved letters clamoring quotes that have been placed here to answer the client's desire to learn French. ●

Architect ·
Marc Whipple AIA

HOPEN PLACE HOUSE

Project Manager / Andrew Takabayashi   **Area** / 446.00 m²   **Landscape Architect** / Paul Robbins   **General Contractor** / Joe Griffith
Structural Engineer / Koje Shoraka, Efficient Consulting Engineers   **Project Manager** / Tom Fanning, Bowery Design & Development
Photography / William MacCollum

The client wanted a complete remodel and update of a mid-century modern on the renowned Bird Streets in the Hollywood Hills. This new owner desired a bold, personally satisfying house, conducive to entertaining Hollywood style, but also required excellent resale potential, as his intent was to sell within two years. His interests were in a residence that maximized the stunning views while combining a sleekly modern aesthetic with an inventive and vibrant use of textures, colors and materials.

The challenge was to create indoor and outdoor living experiences that retained unobstructed views to the horizon line and sky. Our intent was to preserve the integrity of a mid-century classic while rejuvenating the structure with our contemporary uses of color, wood, light and water. The aim was calm elegance and functionality, married with touches of 21st century whimsy as seen in the choice of sculptured art. Water is fully integrated into the design, from the infinity pool, and reflecting ponds, to the wet-edge waterfall along the walkway to the theater. The only spaces not in the original footprint are the Master Bedroom, which floats out at the edge of the property, and the home theater that is tucked in beneath it sharing a wall and windows with the pool. ●

Architect ·
Ippolito Fleitz
Group – Identity
Architects

QUANT 1 APARTMENT

Project Team / Peter Ippolito, Gunter Fleitz, Tim Lessmann, Fabian Greiner, Christian Kirschenmann, Julia Weigle

Client / LBBW Immoblilien Development GmbH   **Location** / Stuttgart, Germany   **Area** / 106 m²   **Photography** / Zooey Braun

QUANT is a luxury, new residential project in a converted 1950s laboratory building in Stuttgart. The exclusive apartment complex is situated in one of Stuttgart's prime residential areas within convenient walking distance of the city centre. To give potential buyers a feel for the multifarious design possibilities inherent in a QUANT apartment, the landlord, LBBW Immobilien GmbH, has commissioned some exceptional model apartments to serve as illustration. Ippolito Fleitz Group has created two unique interiors to complement the building's sophisticated exterior, designed by Wilford Schupp.

Quant 10 was the first model apartment to be realised in 2008; Quant 1 followed suit in 2009. The client commissioned an apartment, whose character would particularly appeal to the target group of single women. Femininity and sensuality thus play an important role in the design and furnishings. Despite its compact layout and clearly defined living zones, the apartment appears extremely spacious, an effect that was achieved through a strong emphasis on transparency and openness in the design of the individual elements.

A glamorous, curved staircase forms the central core of the apartment and opens up the two floors to create an open airspace, around which all the other rooms are grouped. Stepping onto the staircase thus becomes the ideal way of experiencing the apartment in its entirety.

The private rooms, consisting of bedroom, bathroom and dressing room, are nestled together on the upper floor. The bedroom, though a self-contained room in the classical sense, is also open to three sides. The façade wall offers a stunning view to the outside. Opposite the bed, the bedroom opens down onto the dining area via four synchronised windows, with a curtain for when discretion is required. On the other side of the room, an oval window enclosed within a Chesterfield-upholstered seating niche, which creates a sensuous boudoir effect, provides a visual link to the bathroom. The materiality of the bedroom is characterised by soft fabrics: A thick-pile, velour carpet, white, upholstered leather, a diaphanous yet opulent expanse of curtain, and flower motif wallpaper on the wall behind the bed are offset and complemented by off-white bedroom furniture.

The adjoining bathroom is enclosed by porcelain stoneware executed in horizontal stripes, generating a very tactile feel. A mirrored bathroom cupboard of whitewashed oak stretches along the length of the room. With its mirrored doors and multiple illuminated compartments, it exudes a sense of abundance and offers generous storage.

The entrance area of the apartment, which appears twice the size thanks to a mirrored wardrobe, leads directly to the staircase and down into the dining area, which is open over the entire height of both floors. The lofty space is dramatised by three pendant luminaires suspended from the ceiling and a wall of curtains hung all the way down one flank of the room. The dominance of whitewashed oak furnishings on the upper floor is continued in the living and dining areas in the form of a whitewashed parquet floor. A continuous expanse of floor guides the eye towards an open kitchen, which is vis-à-vis the dining table. The kitchen surfaces are solid surface, which contrasts admirably with the retracted, green-varnished glass wall. All in all, natural colours and materials preside throughout the entire ground floor, including the living area. A tall pile of logs and an open fireplace with a concrete lip make a cosy impression, even without a crackling fire in the grate. Firm colour accents have been splashed across the ground floor in the guise of a lilac armchair and structured wallpaper on the staircase wall, which evokes a glass mosaic. In the summer months, the entire ground floor can be opened up to the outside terrace via the large window front. ●

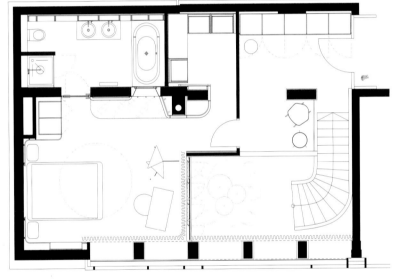

Architects ·
Yunakov Architects

KIEV RESIDENCE

Design Team / Yunakov Ivan, Polina Solovieva   **Client** / Local client   **Location** / Kyiv province, Ukraine   **Built Area** / 600 m²
Plot Size / 3000 m²   **Photography** / Ivan Yunakov

Presented house situated in the Kiev region, on a narrow section near the existing buildings. One of the difficulties of the area was the fact that he has access to water, the river Dnieper. Maintaining all of these regulatory distance, the house had to be placed almost at the very entrance on the territory. In plan, house has a diagonal composition. Just because of the close proximity of neighbors and a good viewing area of adjacent windows, it was decided to create a set of green terraces on the roof to protect against unauthorized viewing.

This object – is the house for the young but already big family, made in the style of 30-ies years. The main objective was to create a bright and open home. Likewise, the principal was to use local materials. That is, a house built entirely of Ukrainian materials (except pottery and lighting).

The house is designed in accordance with the principles of passive design; it is optimally oriented to the cardinal points and takes full advantage of this orientation. This home also responds to many environmental standards, such as: low power consumption, using local materials (savings in transport), green roofs exploited, solid fuel boilers, stand-alone environmental septic, beautiful, warm,

specifications, and of course energy-efficient lighting.

The house has 5 bedrooms (3 children, guest and master), 4 bathrooms, study, theater room, kitchen, and dining room, double-height hall with a fireplace, 4 terraces and a garage for 4 cars. The entire interior is warm, muted tones. Almost all natural materials, the furniture was made according to the sketches of the author of the project and was carried out in Ukraine. The customer family has three children under 7 years old, and to prevent disagreements among them whose room is where and what color, it was decided to make all children's room in the same materials and in one color. And children, in turn, have the opportunity to personalize their own space by the color of diverse LEED-s lights, and of course with lots of toys.

Especially organic and good roof-top terrace where you can relax without fear to be seen neighbors. All terraces have a broad style of gardening, and is designed so that each of the four terraces, flowering in its special schedule in the season, maintaining the brightness of colors throughout the year. ●

1st Floor plan

1. Hall
2. Wardrobe
3. Bathroom
4. Kitchen
5. Dining room
6. Living room
7. Cabinet
8. Cinema
9. Laundry
10. Boiler room
11. Garage
12. Garage
13. Terrace

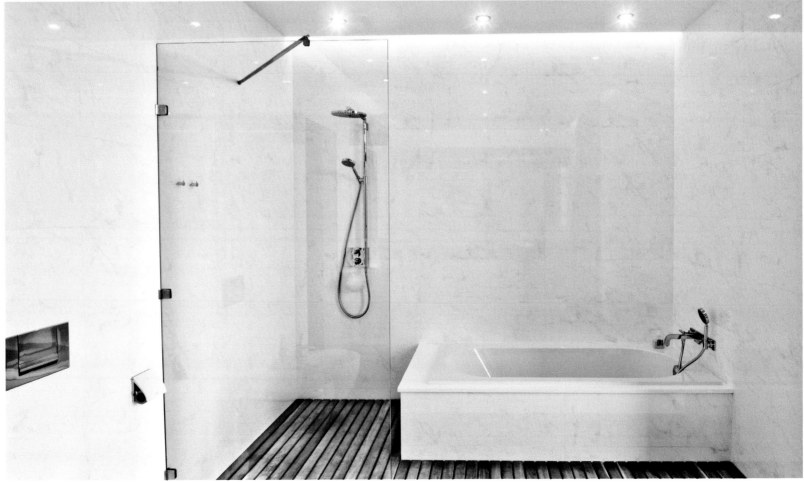

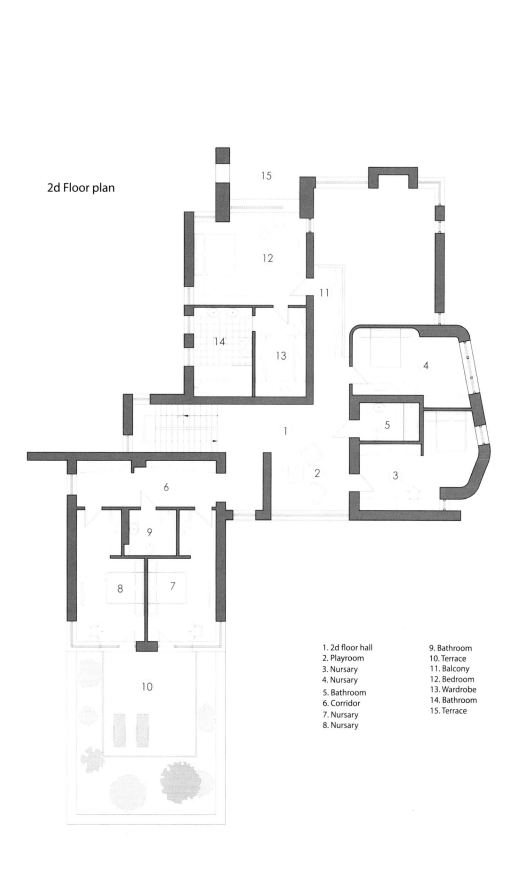

2d Floor plan

1. 2d floor hall
2. Playroom
3. Nursary
4. Nursary
5. Bathroom
6. Corridor
7. Nursary
8. Nursary

9. Bathroom
10. Terrace
11. Balcony
12. Bedroom
13. Wardrobe
14. Bathroom
15. Terrace

Architect ·
Bagnato Architects

1 HUDSON STREET MOONEE PONDS

Location / Victoria, Australia

As both the architects and the client for the project, our brief was to convert a former 120 year old timber church and create an inspiring, artistic & luxurious home that respected the churches spatial qualities, distinct internal features and past history while creating contemporary additions that sat harmoniously together. The site itself measured 18.22m across the front & 22.86m to the side with a total area of 417sqm.

The concept involved retaining the original church that was built to one side of the site. This would allow the creation of a contemporary side addition and a central glazed entry that would form delineation between the old and the new. Of fundamental importance was the retention of as much of the original fabric of the timber church structure & highlight key elements such as the internal timber panelling, trusses & spatial volumes while inserting contemporary design solutions that didn't detract from the church architecture. The use of natural materials throughout the project such as limestone, marble, granite, timber & feature mirrors including recycled timber was part of our philosophy to be true to the material & is a key to the project's success to create a warm & inviting home.

Therefore the design concept involved the manipulation of the spatial qualities of the church by adding mezzanine levels, private rooms & designated areas for modern living without losing the fabric of the church interior. This was achieved with the use of mirrors that reflected existing surfaces, transparent glazed walls and sculptural elements & inserting contemporary finishes, producing a multi-level home that incorporates beautiful rooms that seem to merge with one another to create the most graceful and inspiring space for entertaining and enjoying the ambience of volume and light.

The church space houses an open plan living/meals and kitchen with butler's pantry and formal living/home theatre room with side vestibule with panoramic views of the north- west garden, alfresco area and feature solar heated pool via vast floor to ceiling glazing. A mezzanine level within the volume of the church houses two huge bedrooms with built in joinery opening onto a rumpus room and adjacent bathroom overlooking the living room void and large arched window to valley views of the area. The roof space within the timber trusses of the church has been converted into a New York loft space and is accessed via a staircase in the rumpus area below. It is a multi-functional room with its own kitchenette and private ensuite. Openable skylights and a circular floor to ceiling window encapsulate a panoramic view of the valley & city skyline.

The contemporary adjacent addition is connected to the main church building via a glazed central link housing an amazing basement dining room cellar with polished concrete floor, feature curved re-claimed timber ceiling, mood lighting, floor to ceiling wine racks and a back lit onyx marble wall creating an ambience of absolute luxury. The basement is complimented by an adjacent multipurpose room that can be used as a gym with its floor to ceiling mirrored wall, raised day bed within a cosy wall niche and recessed TV wall. A powder room completes the lower level area.

The ground floor of the contemporary addition houses a double garage with built in cupboards, a large laundry with adjacent laundry chute, a luxury powder room and a guest bedroom that can be used as a study overlooking the garden. The 1st floor is dedicated entirely to the huge master bedroom wing with a walk in robe and entire wall of integrated joinery incorporating TV, desk and window seat all in the ambience of feature lighting. A large adjacent en-suite with free standing bath tub and double bowl vanity unit and floor to ceiling marble & stone completes the theme of a luxury hotel retreat. ●

GROUND FLOOR PLAN

Architect ·
Galeazzo Design

PIED A TERRE A SAO PAULO

Location / São Paulo, Brazil   Area / 90 m²   Photography / Célia Weiss

Located in São Paulo, this 90m² apartment was reformed and received as coating sustainable materials like certified handling wood in the floor and in some walls. The kitchen walls were removed and replaced by an intermixed tone of green olive glass tyle balcony for quick meals. In the side wall there's graffiti of a young artist.

The gray tone of the wood allowed the use of vibrant color like turquoise and humoured decoration. The furniture and decoration itens are a mix of design and vintage furniture, like the green olive leather sofá, the decó armchairs and some fashion universe references like tiedye cushions.

In the dining room there's a pendant shelf with small red spaces that serve as home for a toyart collection and other curiosities. Alongside there's a luminous circular optical object which reinforces the young and relaxed look of the place. The dining table's classical design goes with Constantin Gric chairs. Next to it, serving as a sideboard, there's a dresser painted with a tailoring motif and on top of it a black acrilyc cutted on the form of a classic silhouette.

In the couple suite it is found the same materials choice for coatings and for the chevet was chosen a handmande purple textile that goes with the tartan quilt. Over the bed a thin recess receives a reflected acrilyc cutting. Above that recess italian lamps assists the individual reading while, on the side wall, there's a carved wood sculpture in the form of a wing. ●

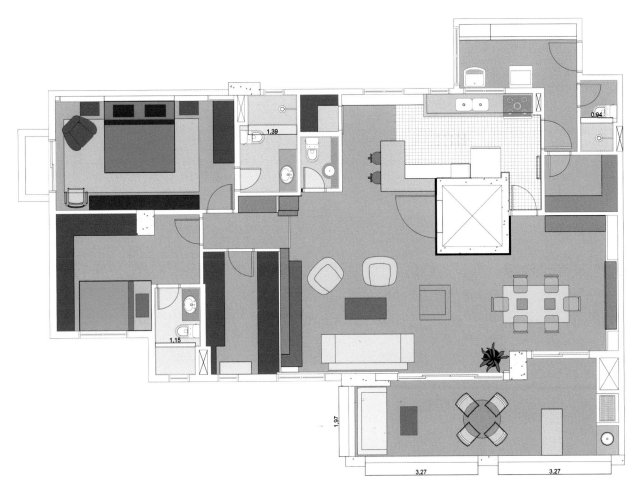

Architect/Interior Designer ·
Hartmann Designs Ltd.

APARTMENT 1216

Main Contractor / Tindall Property Services   **Mechanical Consultant** / Peter Judd Associates   **Electrical Consultant** / LG Bland
Joinery Contractor / Howard Brothers Joinery   **Stone Contractor** / London Marble   **Audio Visual Consultant** / Sound4Vision
Location / London, UK   **Photography** / Richard Gooding (Evening), Tim Young (daytime)

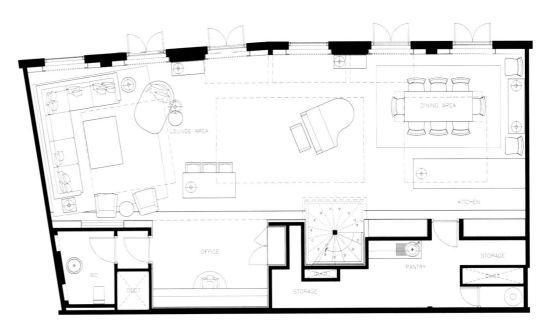

This project originated from the purchase of two penthouse duplex apartments within the prestigious White House Apartments, located in the heart of London's cultural hub at South Bank. Situated on the eleventh and twelfth floors of this magnificent building, the two apartments boast spectacular views out over the Thames and London. We at Hartmann Design's were commissioned, not only as luxury interior designers, but also as architects to engage a lateral conversion of the two apartments into one vibrant and spacious living area. This complete refurbishment and structural reconfiguration had to reflect the dynamism of the modern city, providing a contemporary home with all the conveniences of modern day living. Our first task was to identify the possible constraints on development as the project involved joining the two duplex apartments into one and, with the position being on the eleventh and twelfth floors, there was a considerable amount to review to ensure there was no adverse disruption to the surrounding structure, services and most importantly the neighbors.

Major emphasis within the Client's brief was to create three luxury bedrooms, each with its own en-suite bathroom and a large open plan living, eating, working and entertainment area. The level of finishes and materials throughout the residence were to be of the highest quality, with specialist features aiding a completely modern and elegant way of life.

By introducing a large gallery landing we flooded the space with natural light and illuminated this further with three skylights that are lit by fibre optics creating a starlight effect at night. Imported Arezzo marble from Brazil was used on the floors and floor to ceiling timber paneling on the walls creates a real wow factor entrance. An impressive glass and bronze staircase leads residents down into the living room where they are welcomed by spectacular views over London. The window walls were painted with lambrequins to house hand woven sustainable natural fibre roman blinds. The rear walls are clad in timber panels concealing the utility room, all services and AV equipment. There is an eclectic and unique mix of lighting, creating different moods for each area and for each time of the day and the downstairs cloakroom typifies this with its black granite walls, flooring and gloss black Perspex ceiling. The white porcelain barrel wash hand basin, motion sensor ceiling mounted tap and 'punctuated' lighting really adds to the drama sought after and now is affectionately referred to as 'The Little Night Club'. We designed the entire residence so that it promoted complete open plan living with no visible columns encroaching into the space. Within the kitchen and bar area a monolithic counter was constructed using black granite and a front panel of backlit Carnelian semi-precious stone. Sumptuous and exclusively British custom designed furniture was used throughout, with stylish pieces of furniture from around the world.

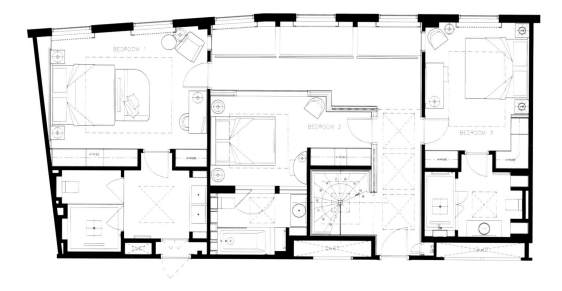

The design of the Master Bedroom exudes pure glamour and comfort with all the modern conveniences. A stunning raw silk headboard wall was created to set off the glamorous tone and beautifully contrast with the black leather upholstered bed and Swarovski crystal embellished scatter cushions. A bespoke dresser and bedside tables with cream leather drawers carry on the sumptuous design positioned on a plush silk carpet with shimmering accents. The master bathroom is accessed through a concealed door and reveals a space that is sophisticated and exciting. The walls are clad in Henry VIII marble and glass walls separate the shower and WC area. The vanity unit is custom designed and manufactured from Corian with a Waterblade shelf above. To set this off, a mirrored ceiling has been fitted creating an illusion of height and space.

The Guest Bedroom boasts a beautiful and natural feel from a combination of natural walnut timber finishes, limestone and woven natural fibre carpets. The use of highly lacquered furniture gives the space a warm and welcoming ambience. Shimmering silk, bronze and ruby fabrics compliment the natural finishes perfectly and strengthen the warm atmosphere. The bathroom was brought into the bedroom to enhance the feeling of space by the installation of a glass wall. Limestone marble from the bathroom was brought through into the bedroom to connect the two spaces further. Specialist and bespoke timber joinery and paneling carries the completely custom and unique feel of this entire residence into every space.

The final bedroom was specifically designed for the client's daughter. We created a delicate feminine room with a cosy feel through the use of warm natural colours and vibrant fabrics. Personalised artwork and quirky accessories were introduced to make the space appropriate and enjoyable for a teenager. A large window takes full advantage of the apartment's idyllic location with dynamic views over the River Thames and the Strand. The en-suite bathroom promotes more natural materials with stunning highly polished Italian marble and natural limestone floor and walls. A beautiful mother of pearl washbasin compliments the timber vanity console with a large walk in shower that is both stylish and practical.

The success of this major project can be attributed not only to our keen interior design eye and exquisite flare, but also to the inner workings of our design process. All design detail; specifications and finishes were agreed prior to commencing any work. The final outcome was decided in the beginning, with the client, to avoid any changes and/or delays during construction that could lead to additional costs. Overall our team successfully achieved what they set out to do from the initial concept stages. Creating a luxurious modern contemporary living space that was designed specifically for the needs and desires of the client. This succinct and bespoke space brought the vibrancy of its eminent residential, business and cultural setting inside, making it a flawless contemporary living space that is perfect for relaxation, work and play. ●

Design Agency ·
Interior Marketing
Group

THE VISIONAIRE —— MODEL APARTMENT

Designers / Cheryl Eisen (President) & Lo Chen (Lead Designer)   Client / The Albanese Organization   Location / New York, USA
Sketch / Lo Chen of Interior Marketing Group   Photography / Rich Caplan Photography

Interior Marketing Group, Inc. designs model homes for new developments in NYC. The Visionaire is located in downtown Manhattan and is the first Condominium in NYC to achieve Leadership in Energy and Environmental Design (LEED) Platinum certification. Interior Marketing Group was hired to design a luxurious yet eco-friendly model apartment, without looking overly "organic".

The design strategy was to create a home that could attract the "uptown buyer" demographic, and to create a feeling of spaciousness in an approximately 1,356 square foot home. INTERIOR MARKETING GROUP creates the feeling of space by applying functionality to every inch of the home, such as adding a floating desk against the large windows, as well as hanging tall mirrors across walls to create an impression of more space and to replicate any light to make rooms even brighter. The color palettes were mostly neutral, to make it more appealing to potential buyers, with pops of color to draw the eye in, both in pictures and in person. Grass cloth wallpapers in dining, living and master bedroom were discriminately and carefully chosen, those made the walls beautifully textured. Custom round dining banquette, media unit, bar unit, and bed headboards were designed for the unique, functional and neutral look of the space.

The results were extremely measurable: the entire line sold out in a matter of weeks, thanks to the model apartment design. ●

Design Agency ·
Interior Marketing
Group

1212 FIFTH AVENUE STAGING

Designers / Cheryl Eisen (President) & Lo Chen (Lead Designer)   **Client** / Durst Fetner Residential   **Location** / New York, USA
Sketch / Lo Chen of Interior Marketing Group   **Photography** / Rich Caplan Photography

Interior Marketing Group was brought in to stage the entire space to attract Buyers. From carefully chosen wallpaper and paint for accent walls, to beautiful drapes, original art, and striking furniture (all from our own warehouse), we created a luxuriously warm and inviting home that Buyers could envision their life in.

To create a stunning space, while keeping a style that had broad appeal, we chose a neutral color palette for paint and created drama using woven grass-cloth wallpaper on a few walls where needed. In the media room we took a risk and painted it a deep brown color to create an updated look of a traditional "study". Overall, the furnishings, accessories, and art, were chosen to create a cohesive set of rooms that dripped with luxury and style. ●

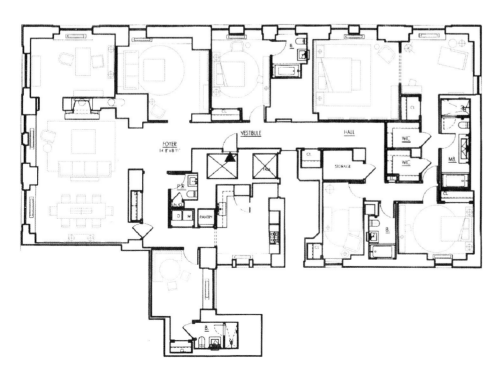

Design Agency ·
ALBUS Design

LEOPARD PROJECT

Designer / Architect Henrique Steyer   **Client** / mid-40s couple   **Location** / Porto Alegre, Brazil   **Photographer** / Marcelo Donadussi

Top international furniture allied with a series of french antique pieces confers luxury and irreverence to this apartment in southern Brazil.

Used to traveling around the world, and therefore with a rich repertoire of cultural references, the young couple who owns this apartment in Porto Alegre wished a distinguished decoration, free from trends and open to the best in world design.

Unusual elements, like pink curtains and impacting artworks make this project with cosmopolitan essence into a very singular one. Top sofas and couches from the Italian Flexform combine with classic items from brands like Poliform and Flos. Contrasting with the contemporary language of the project, a series of antique french furniture completes the decor. Among the artworks, attention is drawn to the one by Mark Gary Adams, a fictional artist created by Henrique itself, with images from 1970s porn movies mixed with playful themes. On the floor, large rugs spread thru the rooms, that also boasts a leopard skin, a marble greek sculpture and a gold-plated entrance door.

On the living room, italian sofas share space with a pair of table lamps by Achille Castiglioni for Flos, and with a dragon sculpture by Lalique. By the dining room, an acrylic side table with italian golden stools serve as support for the barbecue pit. The highlight of this room is the Zeppelin Lamp, designed by Marcel Wanders for Flos. In the hall, the gold-plated door is accompanied by an imposing french mirror next to the elevator.

Still on the living room, Poliform armchairs in eggplant-colored leather make a composition with the golden Rifle Lamp, created by Philippe Starck for Flos. In the dining room, Poliform chairs and dining table next to an artwork from the 'What If?' series, created by Henrique Steyer and digitally manipulated by Felipe Rijo. The image represents the Queen of England with black skin.

On the private living room, a high-gloss cabinet, like the one of the living room Home-Theater, holds a small wine hutch and art objects like a crystal Baccarat panther. An antique english desk is the reading area. In the bedroom, a table and a narrow dresser, both french antiques, serve as nightstands, lighted by white Flos lamps.

In the bathroom, custom woodwork gives a handmade feel to the project. In the washroom, a great collection of antique mirrors line the wall from floor to ceiling. In the kitchen, eggplant-colored cabinets match the cement-colored Corian kitchentop. ●

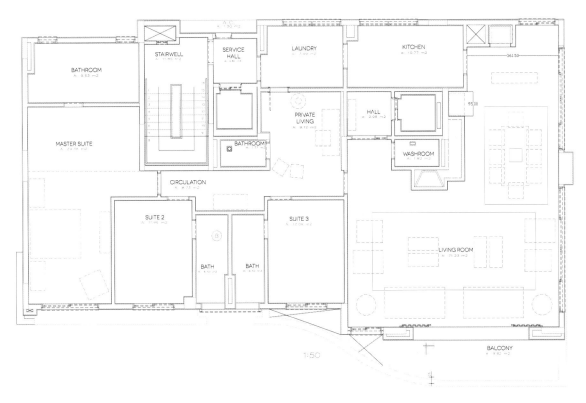

Design Agency ·
Blu Water Studio

THE VALE

Designer / Lai Siew Hong, Mak Sook Har, Nashzelima Ngadmin, Cassandra Sasso   Client / OSK Property Holding Berhad   Location / Sutera Damansara, Selangor, Malaysia   Area / A1 – 194 m^2, A2 – 257 m^2 Photography / James Kuah (Actstudio)

In today's frantic search for a place to live, consumers are faced with the constant bombardment of the newest and latest minimalist trends secretly dreaming of a cozy and comfortable place to call home - without it being too overly cold and futuristic. This is where Blu Water Studio stepped in and approached in the conception of The Vale - successful blend of modern and minimalist, where the organic inspirations brings the warmth touch back to the latest trends.

The outdoor experience are cleverly captured and implemented in the finishes used throughout both the units; the rough surfaces and natural element within the space reinforces the real down-to-earth beauty of the interiors.

In the first townhouse, you will find a private space full of serenity, opulence and pure indulgence.Earthy colors creates an inviting and cozy ambience that brings to mind the respite and comfort one gets from being in the bosom of nature, while the multitude of pure forms are celebrated in the raw materials, creating an overall sense of serene modernity.

Intending to be a dedication to contemporary living, the second townhouse feature strong lines and muted tones, which characterizes the bolder approach in the design.The birth of this concept comes from lying under the tree and staring up at the tree top, at the sunlight peeping through the leaves. The adaptation of shades is expressed in the dramatic finishes with organic materials and monotone nature artworks to form your private intimate urban hideaway.

Disconnected to the world, connected with nature - The Vale provides you with the unique blend of contemporary living and enhanced organic forms. ●

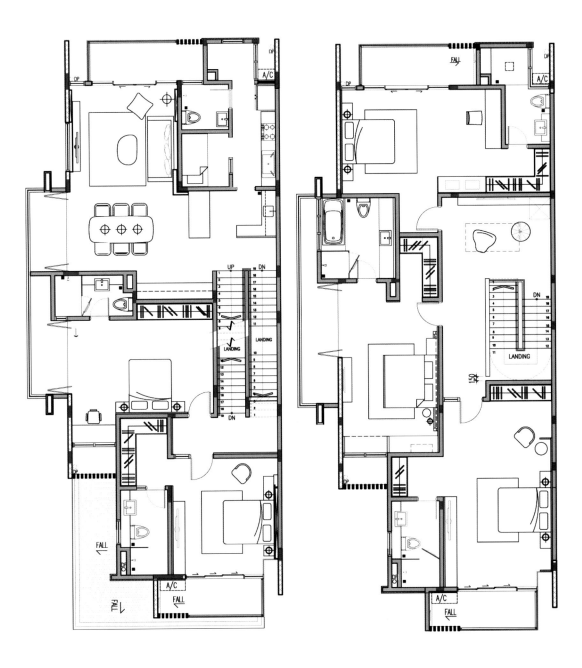

Design Agency ·
Blu Water Studio

6 WESTERN AVENUE

Designer / Lai Siew Hong, Mak Sook Har, Nashzelima Ngadmin, Tan Fang Fang   Client / Belleview Group   Location / Penang, Malaysia
Area / 632 m²   Photography / Keat Song

True luxury means being free. Imagine living freely - in a space to call your own with all the comforts of a private sanctuary, an oasis that soothes the senses from the bustling city and rejuvenates. Free-living means free from all cares and stresses of everyday life, the interior space is the key to mastering this exercise in soothing all the senses. The resort lifestyle is now within reach at 6 Western Avenue, Penang's newest prestigious and privileged address. These bungalows boast spacious 5 bedrooms, 2 living rooms, with a family room and a double volume dining room.

This private retreat is the result of an exercise and restraint - where the idea is to create a living oasis, melting away the fine boundaries between city living and personal sanctuary without it being cold and gaudy. It encompasses open-air concepts where nature and the indoors are allowed to be infused, melting the boundaries between nature and living space.

The feeling of being free is further complimented by the interior decors. At first arrival, you will be greeted by the modern take on a traditional style furniture and accessories. The living room features cool modern furniture, with its sleek and clean lines, allow its users to feel completely at home and seamless with the nature that surrounds them. Naturally, what results is a stark contrast with the dark modern straight lines of the wooden furniture truly inspires a deep sense of serenity as the uncluttered furnishings allow the sights to rest and relax. Each living

space is separated like islands of tropical living - little oasis of cozy spaces that delight the senses. The clever use of the local indigenous hardwood throughout the interior, and in various ways, is a true tribute to the local history steep in culture and local talents. This feature can be found most strongly in the strong lines of the screening around the dining room and family gathering spaces. This screen helps to bring together the coziness of the family.

Being at one with nature is easy as the interiors are tastefully appointed to cleverly integrate the natural elements outside inside like the coconut shell art installation on the dining wall and the orchid design area rug. Textures creates interesting nooks and crannies, cozy corners and come into play via the well-chosen timeless pieces of artifacts and different wall treatments throughout the house. These treatments create layers of interesting spaces to explore and discover. Furthermore, on the second floor there are 3 other bedrooms with individually styled rooms, all perfectly chosen to match the user's personalities while maintaining the resort style integrity. The Master bedroom features a high-sloped double volume ceiling finished in rich local indigenous wood creates a grandiose comfortable atmosphere.

The overall interiors at 6 Western effortlessly inspires the lavish and indulgent lifestyle. ●

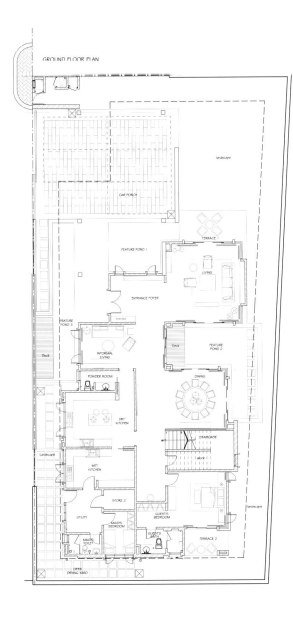

GROUND FLOOR PLAN

Design Agency · Blu Water Studio

THE RESIDENCES

Designer / Lai Siew Hong, Mak Sook Har, Nashzelima Ngadmin, Elaine Yap, Rosabel Yee   **Client** / Tropicana Corporation Berhad
Location / Kuala Lumpur   **Area** / Type A 68m²/732 sqft; Type B 103 m²/1100 sqft   **Photography** / Steak Photography & Khanta Studio

Close your eyes and imagine being a model. Proudly parading on the catwalk during one of the fashion weeks. Dressed in the suit from the latest collection of the world top fashion house, defining the trends for the millions. Now open your eyes and make yourself at home...

Welcome a bespoke design concept in your fashionable living space. The Residences Kuala Lumpur introduce you to the haute couture of sanctuary – high fashion inspired new living trends from the most prestigious catwalks. Either you are fond of the classic and sophisticated style of Christian Dior, or the avantgarde design of Heider Ackermann, glamour will seduce you every time you come home.

The timelessness of Dior defined the vision of the larger apartment (Type B). The spirit of the French designer is expressed both with silhouettes and hues.

Feminine chicness influenced the shapes and textures. Beloved women's pleats, highlighted in the 2012 spring-summer collection, were translated from the catwalk to the apartment as the feature design motif. Pleat-like focal wall in the living area, although made of vinyl timber, took the basic inspiration from the fabric's flexibility. The layering inspired design throughout the apartment was used to create the touch of mystery, which accurate characterizes the fair sex.

To highlight the organic touches, monochrome colours with the dominant black were juxtaposed with vibrant green and powerful magenta. In line with Dior's principle, as he is quoted to say, "I have designed flower women", the bloom chair stands out in the center of living space. This high designer piece in the shape of oversized green flower adds a subtle textural feel to the interior and plays together with the richness of the carpet.

Dramatic ambience created from magenta and black characterizes the space in the bedroom. The intimacy achieved by intensive coloured finishing is enhanced by the layering style of the headboard feature wall. Black tinted mirror with the

enlarged floral pattern is hidden behind metal framing and laser cut metal shelves on the top.

The high fashion mood is further extended in the cozy study room with comfortable seating and chic armchair with footstool. Its black polish surface provides modern take on the classic design paying tribute to the great timeless Christian Dior fashion.

Representing the new designers generation, the unconventional style of Heider Ackermann is perfectly reflected in the smaller apartment (Type A).

According to his fashion shows the vibrant colours were complemented with subtle and monochrome hues. The soothing shades of gray were chosen to interact with the abundant exposure of turquoise and yellow. Tinted mirrors intensify the colour impression and double the sense of spaciousness. The inspiration from the silhouette of Ackerman's clothes determines the vertically cut walls, which elongate the height of the space. Although the living area was very limited, transparent tables and chairs help to open it up. The countless reflections from the soft shaped metallic pendants completed the definitive style. The final touch comes from the sculptural yellow armchair inspired by the diagonal lines of masculine Ackermann design.

Reflective and transparent concept, yet in more subtle way, is further presented in the bedroom. Headboard, being the centerpiece, features stripes of check fabric punctuated with turquoise and yellow tinted mirrors. Together with the prominent framed mirror located behind the desk give the airy feel to the cozy interior. The silhouette and layers concept inspired from Ackerman's fashion is the vision behind the bathroom design. The colored textured glass, which separates it from the bedroom, is used to create shadowed contours – the final touch of sexiness to the space. ●

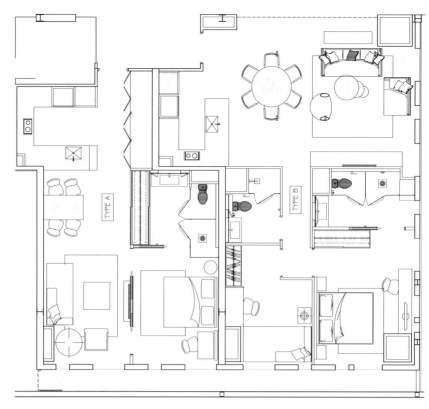

Design Firm ·
Schoos Design

CANON DRIVE HOME

Location / Beverly Hills, California   Area / 836.00 m²   Photography / Matthew Hutchison

When the owners of this Beverly Hills home came to Schoos Design, they had a pre-existing set of plans for a large Mediterranean villa that was ready for building. The only problem was that they didn't like the design anymore -- it was too similar to any number of Spanish or Mediterranean homes in the area and they wanted something different. However, they also did not want to waste all the effort spent creating the plans.

Our solution was to retain as much of the basic structure as possible while reinterpreting the design in a more contemporary way, creating a transitional style between Mediterranean and eclectic modern. Heavy, stereotypically Mediterranean elements such as arches and wrought iron grill work were removed and replaced by square doors and windows and custom designed railings. These streamlined yet subtly curvaceous railings, gates and lighting features bring a clean, modern feel to the exterior.

The more squared-off design also allows for lighter and better sight-lines by creating larger openings for doors and windows. Instead of an imposing, dark archway, for instance, the new front door maximizes the open space. Opening up several rooms to a courtyard just inside the front entrance also enhances flow and brightens the feel of the home. One can see the interior foyer through the front door, creating an inviting indoor/outdoor atmosphere.

The original plans also called for a large, open central atrium with a stairwell and skylight. The challenge of this space was to find a way to bring an organic, personal touch to the cavernous area. There was also a question of what to do to fill acres of white wall space. Our solution was to create a raised plaster relief carving that would ornament the entire atrium and fireplace. The design would be rich and florid with an old-world elegance, but with a white-on-white color scheme that would keep the effect subtle and modern. Creating this unique feature was an involved process that began with a free-hand sketch drawn directly onto the walls, which was gradually embossed with plaster and carved in detail. The end result is a completely original and custom piece of wall art that draws the space together, turning a large white box into an elegant garden. A dramatic chandelier made from strung capiz shells also adds texture and interest to the room.

The eclectic modern approach is continued in the rest of the house, with periodic ornate and sculptural elements adding variety to the clean, minimal design. Vintage furniture pieces are lacquered and upholstered with natural animal hides to give them a more contemporary feel. Organic textures are featured in wood slab tables and other natural artifacts. The indoor/outdoor feeling is also enhanced with large patios and easy access to the large rear garden. ●

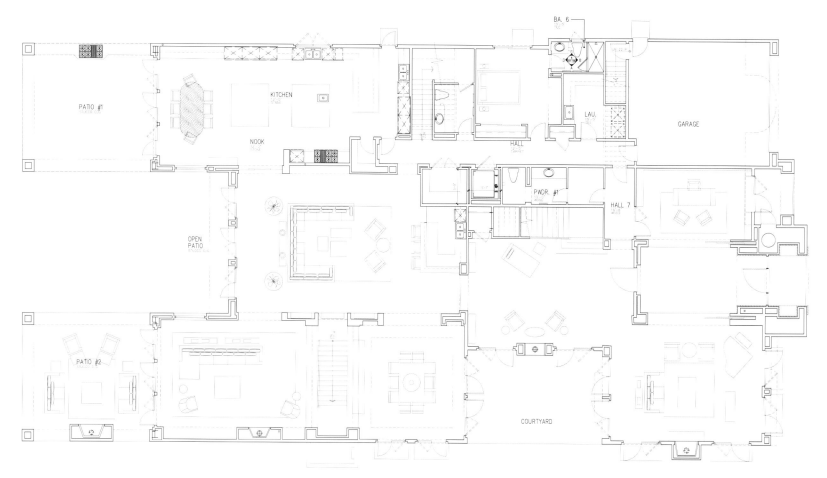

Design Firm ·
Schoos Design

THOUSAND OAKS HOME

Location / Thousand Oaks, California   **Area** / 1,393.00 m²   **Photography** / Matthew Hutchison

The young owners of this spacious home wanted to update the traditional feel of the furnishings and interiors in a way that still reflected the elegance and quality of the architecture and surroundings. There was very little in the way of existing furniture, drapery or other furnishings, and two designers had already been involved whose work had not fit with the clients' tastes or the needs of the house. Our approach was to bring a more contemporary twist to both interior and exterior design, reducing the baroque ornamentation and incorporating more modern furniture and art. Eighty percent of the furniture is custom, designed specifically for the space.

In the two-story living room and atrium, bright white and metallic textures and colors were introduced in the form of upholstery, lighting fixtures, planters and artwork. Patterns are modernist, and furniture and accessories are oversized to fit the scale of the large open room. The crystal chandelier is a custom design featuring stainless steel rings hung in asymmetrically geometric patterns. The two paintings in the living room measuring 20 feet tall, as well as other paintings in the home, are originals painted by Thomas Schoos, the founder of Schoos design, who is an accomplished artist as well as a designer.

The kitchen received a complete makeover including removing the quaint country-style cabinetry and fixtures and replacing them with two-tone gray high-lacquer cabinets and stainless steel Miele appliances. Carved white bone light fixtures add a touch of intricate geometry. In the 2,000 square foot master bedroom, carpets were replaced with walnut hardwood floors. The custom furniture includes intricate details like hand-carved trim on the bed frame and credenzas inlaid with capiz shells and mother-of-pearl. Family rooms and bedrooms for the children were updated with contemporary comfort and the latest technology.

On the exterior, all new landscaping, lighting and patio furniture give the breathtaking California views the feel of a resort. White upholstery carries the theme of the living room outside and into several gracious seating areas around the pool, barbeque and fire pit. ●

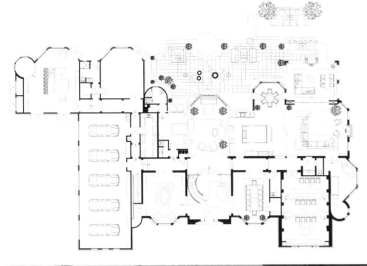

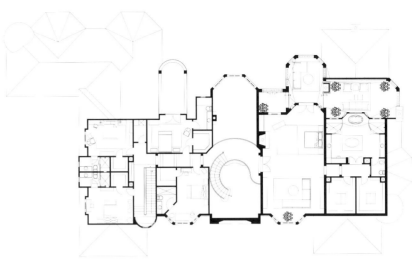

| Architect ·
Oliver Burns | # WALPOLE MAYFAIR APARTMENT |

Location / Arlington Street, Mayfair, London

Walpole Mayfair, is a stunning Grade II building in Mayfair, London has been brought back to life by award-winning architectural interior design and development practice Oliver Burns.

Located in the heart of Mayfair and St James, Grade II listed Walpole Mayfair, dates back to the 18th century and was originally the home of Britain's first Prime Minister, Sir Robert Walpole and his son Horace, eminent patron of the arts.

Walpole Mayfair is an exquisite collection of five exclusive residential apartments. The building has been entirely renovated and all of the period features reinstated, to bring this historical residence back to life. The entirely bespoke design scheme is opulent yet sophisticated and each apartment features three en suite bedrooms, kitchen, reception room and dining room, and is uniquely designed and fitted to the highest specification.

Each of the five luxury London apartments is uniquely designed, with the traditional features of the building complemented by the finest furnishings and finishes. Oliver Burns' elegant styling breathes new life into the building while preserving its rare architectural heritage. With all properties offering three bedroom suites, the apartments on the lower floors have been thoughtfully designed in keeping with their traditional surroundings, whereas those higher up become more contemporary as one ascends the building. The middle apartments, (numbers two, three and four) are lateral in layout, boasting high ceilings and spacious living areas – all dedicated to refined, luxurious living. These are located between a magnificent triplex apartment on the lower ground, ground and first floor of the building and the penthouse on the fifth, sixth and seventh floors which has two roof terraces, the larger with panoramic views of London's most significant landmarks. The most contemporary in style of all of the apartments, it is split over two levels and accessed by lift straight into the open plan living area.

One of the development's highlights is its bathrooms, with rare, hand-sourced, bookmatched marbles, bespoke basins and baths and clever use of lighting. Each apartment incorporates stateof-the-art technology with flat screen televisions discreetly hidden behind mechanised panels, Lutron controlled lighting and Crestron controlled audio and visual controls. The kitchens have Boffi designed cabinetry, offset by dark wood paneling and complemented by luxurious natural stone work surfaces. Bedrooms are sumptuous and beautifully presented; master suites include spacious dressing areas while all have en-suite bathrooms. Oliver Burns has sourced only the best materials and finishes for the homes – ranging from the hand carved white onyx marble washbasin in the penthouse, to the silver and gold gilded ceilings in Number 2 Walpole Mayfair. ●

Architect ·
Lisa Garriss/Plum
Design West

URBAN LIGHT RESIDENCE

Photography / Joe Fletcher

10 NORTH

Award-winning luxury hotel designer Lisa Garriss, president of the Los Angeles-based hospitality design firm Plum Design West, designed this chic, luxury condominium for sophisticated clients who desired a calm refuge from the whirl of Wilshire Boulevard below.

Inspired by the minimalism of Giorgio Armani, with whom she had worked on hotels in Milan and Dubai, Garriss called upon the clean lines and contemporary luxury of the great designer to furnish the 4,000-square-foot condominium.

A pale palette, comprised of ash paneling and subtle linen wall coverings, adds to the sense of serenity, complementing the pale oak furnishings of the new Armani Casa line, while luxurious materials, such as hand-carved Bianco Venetino marble wall panels and sumptuous fabrics, turn what could have been a cold minimalist space into a warm and enveloping Beverly Hills retreat.

A private elevator admits residents to the 10th-floor unit of this coveted building into a stunning lobby sheathed in linen wall covering washed with a light coat of silver leaf. A hand-carved stone wall panel above an Armani console table complete the tableau.

Passing through an ash-paneled entry hallway, one enters the great room, which is outfitted with stunning Armani Casa furniture and lighting, a custom-designed ash-and-lacquer entertainment unit, and an Ahmadi silk-and-wool rug atop a blue Gasgone limestone floor.

Custom designed in a darker wood to contrast with the pale surrounding palette, the Arclinea kitchen designed by Antonio Citterio introduces a sexier mood to the great room.

At the entry to the master bedroom, a custom-designed, low daybed provides a luxurious yet serene space for meditation, reading and relaxing. The ash millwork, combined with the Armani Casa furniture and fabrics of the bedroom, evoke a Japanese feeling.

While the adjoining master bathroom, with its pale palette, ash millwork and Bianco Venetino marble-topped-cabinet atop Lagos Azul limestone floors, feels sexy and luxurious, it continues the quiet, minimalist quality of the home.●

Design Agency · Di Henshall Interior Design	SUNSHINE COAST APARTMENT

Location / Mooloolaba, Queensland, Australia

Di Henshall was approached by the owners of this beautiful Mooloolaba apartment to help them with spatial planning and the integration of some new furnishings, to produce a coherent design concept throughout.

The existing décor was strongly influenced by the clients' love of everything French, which Di used as a starting point.

The existing entry into the hallway was altered and a new chest of drawers with a

mock-crocodile finish was purchased to complement the studded antique double doors already in place. A steel and recycled timber storage box continues the rustic European mood.

New furnishings in the living area, such as the oval black glass topped coffee table, circular side tables with antique silver frames and carved wooden table lamps are set against a dramatic backdrop of duck egg blue wallpaper. Custom white acrylic panels with a daisy floral motif provide a three dimensional focal

point. This room is a bright, fresh and a lovely contrast to the recycled furniture in the entry and hallway.

New taupe wallpaper with a fleur-de-lys pattern in the master bedroom provides a striking backdrop for the new bedding and the mahogany framed circular mirror. Two oversized champagne coloured blown glass table lamps complete the picture.

Additional soft furnishings, such as the scatter cushions with French script, a new custom made ottoman in the media room and new kitchen bar stools were selected to reinforce the design intent, along with decorative accessories such as a white resin stallion and diamond cut crystal hurricane vases.

The clients' comment at the conclusion: "...thanks for the wonderful job you've done with our apartment. We absolutely love the final result and the wallpaper is just awesome". ●

Architects ·
Whipple Russell
Architects

GRANDVIEW DRIVE

Location / Hollywood Hills, California   **Area** / 372 m²

This was a challenging remodel/ recreation, as the lot is very long and narrow; and existing walls of the old structure controlled choices. Our client, a successful model, required living space that worked for entertaining as well as providing a quiet retreat for guests. The house is oriented on the north/south axis, with an angled 'slice' taken out of the view-side of the home, drawing your eye towards the ocean and the setting sun. A centrally located "glass box" switchback staircase was designed for egress from the first floor all the way up through the levels of the home to the rooftop. The staircase is a very functional piece of art. All was accomplished; keeping in mind, shape, usability, light, and of course, the views. Contemporary meets modern; a three-story ship with roof deck on top. ●

Architect ·
Nasciturus Design

GRZYBOWSKA APARTMENT

Photography / Yassen Hristov

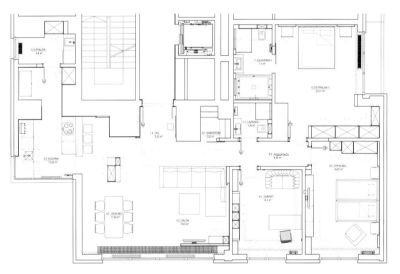

This apartment located in the very center of Warsaw was designed for a gentleman often visiting the city on bussiness.

The project perfectly matches stylish look with full functionality. Original solutions come along with solid and one of kind materials, such as Emperador stone and Aqua TV used in the bathroom, make the interior even more attractive. The timeless classic weaving with contemporary glamour can be noticed in every single room which makes the whole apartment a coherent whole.

The combination of neutral colors, glistening surfaces and eye-catching fabrics well noticed in a living room is a smart way to make the interior a remarkable place to live in. ●

Architect and
Interior ·
ARCO Arquitectura
Contemporánea

DEPARTAMENTO ASL

Project Team / José Lew Kirsch, Bernardo Lew Kirsch, Oscar Sarabia, Jesús Román, Jonathan Herrejón, Miguel Ocampo, Nahela Hinojosa, Federico Teista, Guillermo Martinez, José Ruiz, Gerardo Fernández, Beatriz Canuto   **Building and construction supervisión** / ARCO Arquitectura Contemporánea   **Location** / México D.F.   **Area** / 643 m²   **Photography** / Jaime Navarro

For the design of this apartment, located west of México City, the most important was to find the appropriate design language to balance the contemporary space with the classic furniture. For this a finishes palette and sober and elegant colors were selected to allow the styles fusion.

The space is divided into living and study, both separated by a small living used for informal meetings. The dining room is in a separate room that has also magnificent views, a grand chandelier in the center of the space and connects directly with services. The result is a contemporary space with an atmosphere in which the taste for the classic defines its special personality. ●

Architect project
and Interior ·
ARCO Arquitectura
Contemporánea

DEPARTAMENTO CGB

Project Team / José Lew Kirsch, Bernardo Lew Kirsch, Oscar Sarabia, Jesús Román, Jonathan Herrejón, Miguel Ocampo, Nahela Hinojosa, Federico Teista, Guillermo Martinez, Beatriz Canuto   **Building and construction supervision** / ARCO Arquitectura Contemporánea   **Location** / México   **Area** / 610 m²   **Photography** / Jaime Navarro

The creation of atmospheres that are suitable for every space, enhancing the harmony that integrates the entire project, is the guiding principle that defines the project done by ARCO Arquitectura Contemporánea for this apartment in Mexico City. Its privileged location provides, beside the fantastic views, a pleasant surrounding suitable to integrate the outdoors to the interior project.

From the entrance, the open spaces and generous double height of the public areas are distinguished in an elegant and contemporary ambiance that goes through the living room, dinette and dining room delimited by the main corridor and the large window that separates the interior from the terrace. For the whole house custom designed and made furniture as well as from important Italian brands were used. The natural color palette plays with the dark color accents that were selected to integrate the inhabitants personality in each space. ●

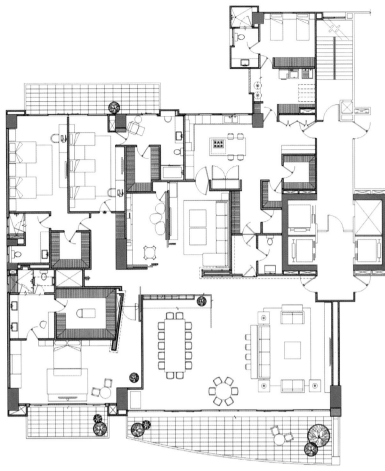

Architect ·
Caballero Design

BELGRAVE HOUSE

Location / London, UK   Photography / Andrew Beasley

Caballero Design felt that it was essential that design started with the front door. So they designed a completely new door set and by removing the window above the doors they were able to accommodate a 2.4 meter tall dark oak door which they then framed with a pair of windows to either side. Internally the full length windows allowed the light from outside to travel over a much longer distance reflecting off the polished floor.

In their approach they designed a geometric pattern for the floor consisting of the soft white Brillante marble contrasting with the dark brown Port Laurent marble.

The doorways to the adjoining rooms were all raised from standard height to add grandeur and the existing doors replaced with ebony veneered doors. To compliment these imposing doors the natural oak staircase was French polished to match and then was softened with a silk runner along the centre of the treads.

The main drawing room is elegantly furnished with silk and velvet upholstery providing warmth and texture. To give the room flexibility for both formal in informal occasions a television was discreetly installed behind a special two way observation mirror which clads the chimney breast.

Upstairs, their designs produced a suite that spanned over four rooms comprising of the main bedroom, dressing room, private lounge and bathroom. In the master bedroom the oversized bed backs onto a wall fully upholstered in buttoned silk panels. Ornate silver lamps add an air of decadence to the subtle handmade ebony side tables. For the master bathroom they selected a stunningly elegant Castello freestanding bath to be the focal point with its curves traced by a striking elliptical wall, tiled with a pearlescent Bisazza mosaic. The private lounge provides an ideal space to retire in the evenings and special consideration was given to feel of the materials along with its appearance under low lighting. From the elegant reflections cast by the silver leaf paper lining on the chimney breast, to the movement in the silk velvet fabric, this room contains has an alluring opulence. Adjoining the private lounge is the master dressing room. The fitted wardrobes and dressing table features rich dark oak frames, doors and drawers with soft inset fabric and elegant Murano glass handles. Design cues from high-end fashion boutiques add a sense of occasion such as silk curtains, rather than doors to close off the room and a glazed central display cabinet to revealing ties, silk scarves and other accessories.

As the final part of the scheme they chose to locate a purposeful home cinema in one of the loft rooms. Unfortunately the room had a typically irregular shape with steeply eaved ceiling, recessed dormer window and stepped return walls. Incorporating information from the AV specialist in relation to acoustics, their designs centred around a dramatic hardwood slat ceiling with discrete storage concealed along the return walls. The result was that the previously awkward roof angles were replaced with the elegant tapering lines of a clamshell ceiling reminiscent of a more decadent era. In contrast to the dark slat ceiling the walls and the doors to the concealed storage were upholstered in silk. The final piece de resistance was the inclusions of a subtly lit wet bar and drinks cooler within the panelling. With the clients wish to keep the space strictly informal they avoided arranging the room with rows of typical cinema chairs and instead commission a set of oversized armchairs upholstered in leather and finished with a cosy faux fur throw. ●

Architect ·
Craft Arquitectos

Location / Col. Bosques de las lomas, Mexico   **Area** / 235 m²

The architectural concept of the department is based on the integration of movement spaces heights, materials and lighting.

The zoning of space becomes fragmented through solid blocks of varying heights that define the different areas within the department, these elements make up the private and service areas such as restrooms and locker.

After passing the threshold of the door, the perceived location of each department spaces is almost immediate. I feel social areas early surprise the user in the correct composition exists through a compositional axis by a main hall, which by its hierarchy, divides the important areas of the department, likewise, the walls

that define the spaces do not reach the level of slab to reveal the continuity and achieve greater amplitude in a comfort zone.

Light, plasticity and functionality come together in perfect balance with the materials used (wood, glass, stone and steel) governing delimiting elements to create different environments within the same space. The view outward becomes a main element for composition and integration within the spaces of most importance, being the fundamental natural lighting for effect emphatic in those areas. ●

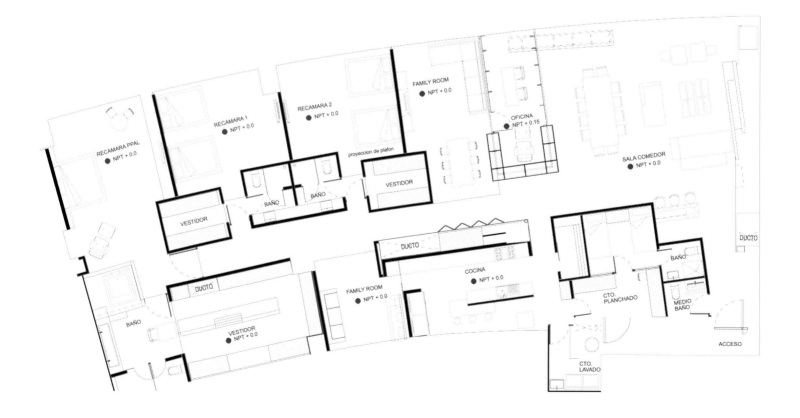

Architect ·
Craft Arquitectos

TB-1602

Location / Bosques del Olivo, México   Area / 425 m²

Located in Bosquesdel Olivo, west of the State of Mexico, Torre Bosques is a project designed to the needs of local residents which are based on live, work and interact. All this is achieved through the interaction of different spaces interlinked through materials, furniture and height changes.

Designed with large spaces, where the furniture and art were perfectly selected to generate greater comfort and harmonyin each of the areas of the department.

Walls covered with wood in its natural state as well as providing warmth and functionality are perfect places to suit the furniture, the green wall the covers more than 7 meters high with the water surface below creates a perfect transitional space where they connect the kitchen and dining, brick and gray base finish on

the walls of the room that creates a contrast study with white tones of the furniture, as well as aluminum and glass confined to form a perfect relationship inside outside giving a spectacular view.

The lighting is rather direct and indirect radiating the space organically; indirect light creates warm spaces in certain areas and gives a contrast between the walls and furniture to produce different scenes and versatile spaces for the user.

The predominant materials in the apartment are marble, wood, steel and in conjunction with natural light create a harmonious composition emphasizing each of the areas. ●

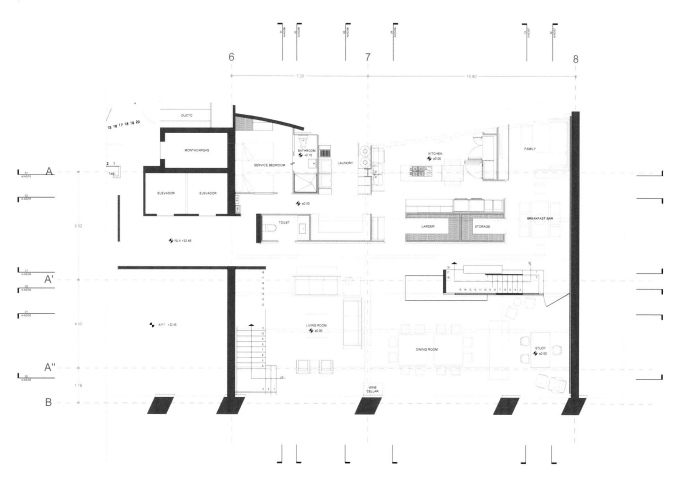

Architects ·
Halo Design
Interiors

AN IMMACULATE HOME IN OXSHOTT

Location / Weybridge, UK   Photography / Robert Sanderson

The clients, a professional couple with two young boys, were keen to stamp their mark on their new home, ensuring that it fulfilled the way they like to live. Their brief was to update the house generally, focusing in particular on the master suite, to include a completely new bathroom and dressing room areas. They also put the spotlight on the new library area with a view to creating a private study space, but at the same time ensuring that there was room for the whole family to spend time together in the space.

Halo's ideas focused on taking the best elements of the existing interiors and blending them with new schemes to reflect the clients' lifestyle.

As you enter the property a two storey atrium style hallway features Bocci pendant chandelier which hangs down above spanning two floors. Immediately ahead is the formal dining room which can comfortably seat ten. The formal semi open plan connecting sitting room is off to the right where a rare grand piano takes pride of place next to the fireplace.

All the ground floor rooms that directly face the rear garden are sunken, two steps down off the main ground floor, to give definition to the spaces and make them feel grander. These rooms include the dining room, family room and media room.

The kitchen by Mowlem incorporates concealed appliances with an eat-in dining table for owner's small children and bar stools for the adults and guests.

Leading off the kitchen is the large sunken family room with doors opening directly onto the stone patio. A family media room for watching films on comfortable lounging sofas also leads off from the kitchen. A utility room and playroom are also located on the ground floor.

Upstairs, the challenging skeilings in the library located above the garage were minimised by the use of quarter cut oak joinery, dark stained, cladding the room in built-in shelving, back lit, to ensure a relaxing environment. Special attention was given to the client's chess board, which sits in pride of place in the library area, as this was a particular activity the owner enjoys sharing with his children.

The master bathroom was completely re-configured to provide a large walk-through shower, clad in bronze tiles, with bronze frames used as a feature around recessed light boxes and mirror cabinets above the bespoke double vanity unit.

The dressing areas were another challenge due to space restriction and skeilings. Halo overcame the challenges by working with the clients to create simple lacquered wardrobes, with a back-lit Perspex shoe stand taking pride of place, giving the client an important display for her varied and valued shoe collection. ●

Architects ·
Telemak Ananyan,
Gohar Isakhanyan,
Arus Manvelyan

APARTMENT DESIGN ON MARSHAL KATUKOV STR.

Location / Moscow, Russia   **Area** / 113.0 m²

The main concept for the project was to create a comfortable and functional space with elements of luxury.

Pastel colors were chosen as a main palette for the hallway, living room and dining room. Colorful paintings of Armenian artists create some accents in the rooms. The floors are made of porcelain of the Portuguese manufacturer "Revigres". The walls in the living room are decorated with paintings, decorative plaster and tile inserts.

A lot of wood is used in the interior of the bedroom. The rich texture of the wood creates a cozy atmosphere in the room.

The home-office is also implemented with ecological materials. Decorative panels of walnut wood highlight the importance of the main element of the cabinet - the workplace. A special interior decoration is the rosewood flooring, made by special order.

Teak wood was used for the floor and one of the walls in the master bathroom. Teak wood is one of the most precious woods in the world, it has an expressive texture, golden- brown shade with glitter effect and unique features that made that kind of wood popular in a variety of fields - from shipbuilding to interior and landscape design. Teak floors have the ability to store and release heat, which is very important to maintain a comfortable temperature in the bathroom, in addition, unlike the ceramic tiles, teak floors do not slip when getting wet. This durable, long-lasting and very beautiful kind of wood brings motives of true luxury in the interior.

The remaining walls are made with natural travertine tiles with inserts of semi-precious stones from the collection of the Italian company "Antolini Luigi".

The second bathroom is decorated in warm tones of coral and milk .Tiles of coral and milk travertine from the Italian factory "Cottoveneto" are used in the interior.

Products of the Swiss sanitary ware factory "Laufen" and taps of the German company "DornBracht", assembled by hand are used in the interior of the bathrooms.

Furniture of the leading manufacturers "Cattelan Italia", "B & B Italia", "Poliform", "MisuraEmme", "Minotti" and lighting fixtures of famous factories "Vistosi", "Artemide", "XAL", "Vibia", " OnoLuce "," Armani "," Schmitz Leuchten " are used in the interior. ●

Architect ·
Kurt Krueger
Architect

WESTGATE RESIDENCE

Location / Los Angeles, CA, USA   General Contractor / Rhino Construction Group, Inc.   Photography / Unlimited Style Photography

The Westgate Residence is a renovation of a 1948 house located in Brentwood, CA where the objective was to architecturally update the building through the use of new materials, spatial definition and openings, but without increasing the overall square footage or building envelope.

As a design-build collaboration with Rhino Construction Group, Inc the design process was fluid, allowing for discovery and adaptation during the construction process. Situated near a fairly busy street intersection with an abundance of foot traffic, the challenge was to create a peaceful dwelling from an existing building shell. Because the home owners are a retired couple, ease of function and overall practicality were just as important as the overall design. Our mission was to seamlessly blend these requirements in a poetic way.

Rather than adding more area with a second floor, the house was kept to one level. The 50'x100' lot meant that the existing footprint has already been maximized,

providing a first floor area at 2,200 square feet. However, the house had good bones, allowing us to pierce new window, door, and skylight openings, providing more natural light. Walls and unnecessary partitions were removed, allowing the main area to feel as one large space, but within it, containing smaller zones.

Security was an important factor to consider along with the limited outdoor space, so a courtyard with retractable sunshades was created to enclose the front yard. Douglas fir wood slats are placed at such a height that those on the sidewalk level cannot see in.

The heightening of the senses was important throughout, and informed the selection of rich materials with tactile qualities. Attention to details creates unique elements of surprise and wonder to the small space. Fountains and water elements add white noise to reduce the sound of street traffic while the landscaping was designed to screen, yet give a sense of calm and reflection. ●

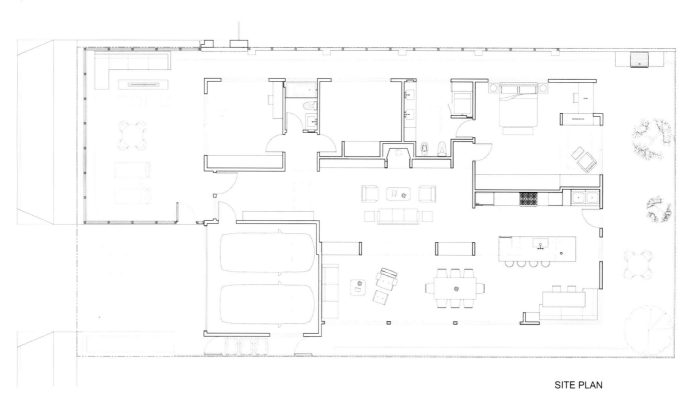

SITE PLAN

Architects ·
MSWW
Magdalena
Konopka, Marcin
Konopka

SEA TOWERS APARTMENT

Location / Gdynia, Polska   Photography / Marcin Konopka (MSWW)

The investor had a wish to design a luxerious weekend apartment that could at the same time be used as an every-day home. We've received a task to design an apartment from its basics: the investor handed us an open plan of 100m2 that we were supposed to design. Functional and aesthetic guidelines that we've received let us design an interior of clear division on common and private space. The common part consists of a living room with kitchen annex. A spacious hall leads to a study/guest-room separated by sliding glass door. There are closets that hold pieces of home equipment in the hall. The private space is — at the first glance

— invisible: together with a little bathroom it's hidden behind the door that was integrated with wall lining. A bedroom with wardrobe and a bathroom are parts of the private zone.

Economy of colours and the leitmotif of white was a suggestion of the investor and a result of our perception of this specific, inspiring space, where the Baltic Sea plays the main role. Thanks to big windows in the living room, the apartment became a space of integrated inside and outside views.

The line of custom furniture under the window repeats the landscape and continuous on the perpendicular wall. In order to minimize objects in the space, the whole necessary equipment had been hidden there — it holds a canal heater, that together with side surfaces creates a seat with a beautiful view. Soft pillows are very welcoming. The furniture also holds AV system, subwoofer and a bio fireplace located on the perpendicular wall. Above a TV set hidden behind a black glass panel is situated — the panel also protects the wall from the fireplace's warmth. The composition can be described as reserved and respectful to the landscape outside. Our graphics gives background to the dark monolith.

Few pieces of orange furniture and décor are contrasting accents in the investor's most favorite colour.

Very important part of the interior is the custom furniture — thanks to it the space is both aesthetically coherent and functional.

After sunset, when the Baltic becomes disturbingly dark and only few lights spark on the waterfront, the apartment gains a new life. Thanks to carefully chosen light and system of intelligent steering we can create light scenes with ease and pleasure. After dark horizontal divisions become more visible thanks to the hidden light and the fire bringing cosiness. Although there are a lot of white surfaces and lustrous textures, the apartment is pleasantly warm and welcoming. ●

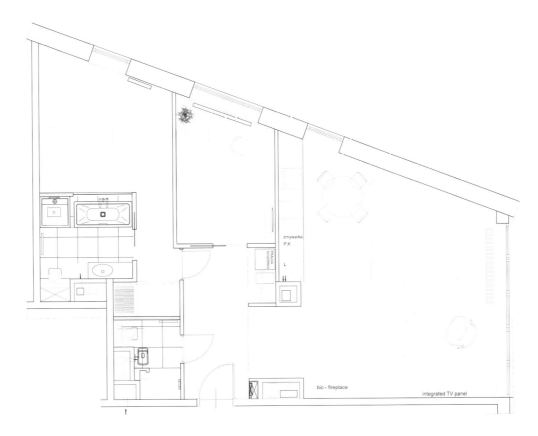

MSWW_ Apartment in Gdynia, Sea Towers

Architect ·
Rolf Ockert
Design

BRONTE HOUSE

Client / Private   Location / Bronte, Sydney   Builder / Brianda Projects, Jesse Gooch   Photography / Sharrin Rees

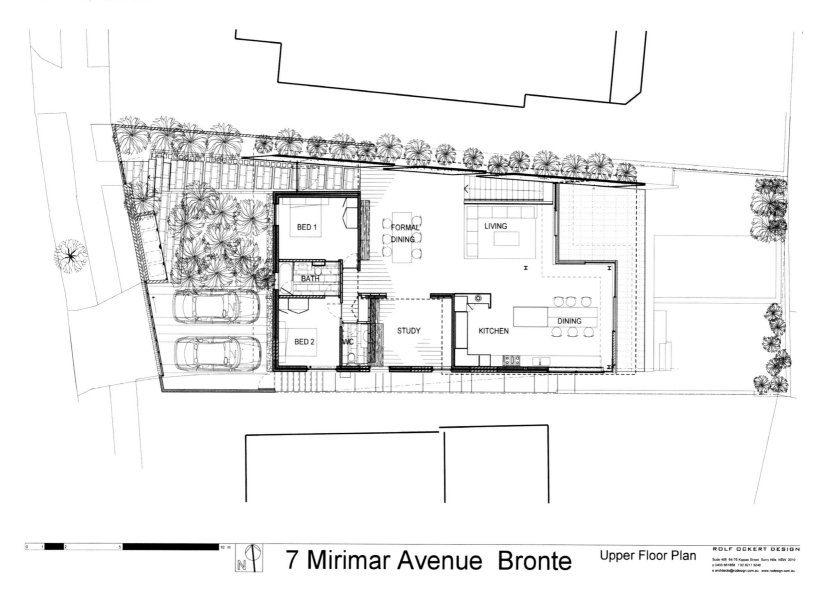

7 Mirimar Avenue Bronte   Upper Floor Plan

ROLF OCKERT DESIGN
Suite 406 64-76 Kippax Street Surry Hills NSW 2010
p 0400 661858 f 02 8211 5246
e architects@rodesign.com.au www.rodesign.com.au

The client approached us to create house of their dreams on a site perched high over the Pacific Ocean, a home that was to make them feel like being on holiday every day. While the view was fantastic the site was very small and suffocated by overbearing neighbouring dwellings.

The finished house, though, feels generous and as if it is alone with the ocean and the sky.

Being tightly restricted by site conditions there were only two avenues we could take to create generosity of space and location: Firstly the surprising height of the living room space that takes advantage of the only extravagant spatial dimension available to us.

And secondly the pursuit of sightlines to water and sky wherever possible. High side walls, for privacy but also to provide mass for a comfortable indoor climate, have continuous highlight windows for the enjoyment of 360° views of the sky. The large face concrete wall dominating the space has slim slot windows, allowing teasing glimpses of the ocean when entering the house while effectively cutting out the visual presence of the neighbour.

The house opens itself up completely to the East, the presentation of the stunning water views.

This also allows the capture of the constant ocean breezes to cool down the house throughout the year, easily regulated by a plethora of ventilation options from sliding doors to operable louvres.

A rich but reduced palette of strong, earthy materials, from the above mentioned concrete to Timber flooring and ceilings, rust metal finishes and thick, textured renders, contrasts with the fine detailing of the interior and anchors the residence against the airy, light aspect created by the opening to the views.

Sophisticated simplicity would be the most appropriate motto for the design of this house. Being on a very small block the client's expectations of the generosity and design standard to be achieved required a very stringent approach. While the focus is naturally on the maximisation of the enjoyment of the majestic ocean views it was the suburban context that drove most of the major design decisions: The slotted northern concrete wall, the solid southern facade, the high roof with its continuous strip of highlight windows and louvres. ●

Architect ·
Rolf Ockert

FAIRFAX AVENUE APARTMENT

Location / Bellevue Hills, Sydney   Furniture and Decoration selection / Nerida Bawtree   Builder / Brianda Projects   Photography / Sharrin Rees

We were approached by a bachelor who had just bought a penthouse apartment in an upmarket suburb of Sydney's East. The apartment occupied the entire top floor of a 1940's building and had great views over Sydney harbour. On the downside it was not very well laid out and the living area was small. The connection of the living area as well as access to the large terrace was also not ideal.

We therefore proposed a mixture of major building work in one, living, part and minor corrections in the other, bedroom, part of the apartment. The former wall to the terrace was removed completely and replaced with a glazed extension that not only enlarged the critical living room area but also allowed a wide panoramic view as well as enjoyment of the existing mature trees.

The interior layout is defined by full height, gently sweeping "spine" wall of dark African Wenge wood veneer. This element connects the entry and the living area and leads the visitor into the heart of the apartment's living area and rectifies the previously disorienting organisation of the apartment.

Several existing internal walls were removed to make the Kitchen/Living area as generous as possible. An existing widening in the corridor was integrated in the living zone as a bar area for the wine loving client. The resulting sequence of spaces, starting from the entry, guided by the soft 'flowing' veneer clad spine wall, results in an apparent spatial generosity beyond its actual square meterage. A "ribbon" of custom made joinery, containing a multitude of uses, follows this sequence of spaces on the wall opposite the spine, thus tying the spaces together. Due to this common element the spaces are read as connected and belonging together. The shape of that joinery ribbon also enhances and emphasises the outline shape of the existing apartment walls.

The veneer was chosen as Pacific Walnut, lighter and more lively grained than the Wenge on the wall to give this element its own independence and playfulness.

The Kitchen is partly hidden behind the veneer wall. AAS a result the more utilitarian zones, fridge, ovens etc are not dominant from the living space while the benches, preparation areas are in direct contact with the living and Dining areas. The shapes again help to soften the transitions between zones and to be read in conjunction with other elements as a family of new insertions versus the existing.

The layout of the Bedroom part of the apartment was left largely as existing, with minor adjustments. All new built-in joinery picks up on design clues and materials from the living part of the apartment to ensure continuity.

The terrace decking and new steel balustrade extension, required by modern building regulations, are ostentatiously "Ocean liner style", a reference to not only the era and style of the existing apartment block but also the magnificient views of Sydney Harbour. ●

Architect ·
SHH

WEST LONDON HOUSE

Location / Holland Park, London   **Area** / 929.00 m²

SHH completes new-build West London House with stunning pool and leisure facilities. The new house is now made up of five stores: the lower-ground level (housing the pool and leisure areas); the family-orientated garden level (which opens directly out to the garden space and barbeque terrace at the rear via bi-folding 2.4m x 4.5m glass doors leading out from the main family living space); the upper garden level, which includes the formal reception room and roof terrace and a first and second floors, where most of the bedrooms are located.

As well as being architects on the scheme, SHH also planned all the interiors and designed all the joinery, lighting design, ceiling, wall and floor finishes, whilst all loose furniture and artworks were created or sourced by South African designer Craig Kaplan.

The formal reception room is dominated by a feature joinery wall in stained oak, with a stone plinth and a column and further plinth in dark emperador marble set in front of it, that house a dumb waiter system (hidden behind a sliding panel) and fireplace respectively. The feature wall has inset cavities for the display of sculptural white vases. For the room's lighting scheme, lamps are used to create a

sense of intimacy (and to keep the ceilings clean), with the exception of two stand-out pendant fittings. The pendants, which use black, mirrored nickel shards to stunning effect, are by designer Tom Kirk. One is a standard size (over the table in the study area), whilst the other, over the dark wood, ten-seater dining table, was created to bespoke dimensions for this project.

The formal living space links, through the bay window, to an outdoor terrace facing over the rear garden for use whilst entertaining (or for the use of guests who smoke) First and Second Floors. The stair leading up to the bedrooms at the first and second floor levels is quite traditional, reflecting the other formal touches to the front of the house, with white-painted timber spindles and a French polished oak handrail. A stunning Bocci chandlier light hangs down into the stair void, with glass bauble lights at varying levels providing a spectacular piece of theatre in an area that is often overlooked.

At the first floor level, a glass balustrade overlooks the lobby area to ensure as many sightlines are kept open in the house as possible. This floor houses the master suite to the rear of the space, facing onto the garden. Currently there is a

guest bedroom also on this floor, which features built-in joinery (created by Hannah Contracts) and wallpaper by Tektura and an en suite bathroom with curved walls made of calacatta oro marble mosaics (also used on the floor), but there also is the capacity for the master suite to extend over the whole floor once the kids have left home.

The master bedroom features his'n'her wardrobes, which are accessed by a door to either side of the bedhead. The bedroom itself has an upholstered wall behind the bed to serve as a bed head, whilst a television is recessed into joinery opposite, clad in matching upholstery. Three children's bedrooms are located on the top floor of the house. All are en suite and benefit from plenty of natural light from the skylights above.

The first level down is the garden level, where the main family living areas are located in an open space created according to 'lateral living' principles. The space is comprised of the main Bulthaup kitchen (supplied by Kitchen Architecture), with units created in walnut with an aluminium finish, along with a stainless steel island and a hidden dumb waiter system set behind the Bulthaupunits, which links

to the formal reception room on the upper ground floor. Immediately beyond the kitchen area is a breakfast table and chairs and then, within the extended glass box section of the rear elevation, an informal family seating and television area with sofas, tables, lamps and easy chairs. Italian limestone flooring leads outside through the bi-folding doors to connect to the barbeque terrace.

Alongside the pool sits a glass box gym area, with Bolon flooring and a rear wall in oiled cedar slats. A stand-out corridor links this area to the sauna, steam room and changing rooms, bordered by a fretwork wall, which was chosen for the shadows itcreates from the natural light coming into the corridor and which is made up of fire-rated glass screens with fretwork panels in front of them.

The cinema and media room, which has iPad-based Savant controls for lighting and music (which can also be used for all other rooms in the house) and an almost-invisible projector, set into the air conditioning grille accessed from the room behind, so that only the lens is visible.

Architects ·
Tamara Magel
Design

GIBSON LANE

Location / New York, USA   Photography / Yale Wagner

Gibson Lane is located in one of the most expensive zip codes in The United States, with the country's largest and most expensive home situated just around the corner. This traditional shingle style 7,000 sq. ft. five bedroom home is located on the coveted Gibson Beach, opposite singer songwriter Billy Joel's x wife, with views of the Atlantic Ocean from all three levels.

The house was newly built in 2010 and Magels' client was the first owner. The homeowner lives there almost full time but wanted their home to feel relaxed, but also glamorous and sophisticated enough to be their main residence. With a neutral pallet and clean lined furniture as the base, the home's interest is in the texture and eclectic mix of styles. With a budget of $2m also Tamara was able to be indulgent in what she chose for the interior.

Phillip Jeffrey's grey grass cloths wallpaper and Farrow & Ball's Parma Blue paint set the feel and tone, while the mix of limestone parchment and leather add depth and structure. Key pieces of classic 1960's furniture and lighting add strong focal point interest. The Hans Wagner hammock chaise and chair in the lounge add the beach feeling while maintaining the exclusivity of the home. And all other interior design and adornments also add the modern flair, fashion accents to the house.

Structural work occurred on the 2nd floor where Magel converted a 6th bedroom into a spacious dressing area and closet, while a further additional bedroom was converted into a library for the client's collection of treasured books. All the bathrooms were upgraded at the same time.

Lighting throughout plays an important role in the house. To sum up, Magle's

eclectic eye transformed this wonderfully positioned home into a showcase of modern flair, fashion accents, and bohemian edge, with the sophistication necessary and expected for the Hamptons, the vacation home for New Yorkers and the privileged, but still relaxed enough to sit on Gibson beach. ●

Architect ·
Toth Project
Architect
Office

LAKESIDE HOME IN BALATONBOGLAR

Interior Design / István Bényei   **Location** / Balatonboglár 8630, Hungary   **Photography** / Zsolt Batár

House Area / 335 m² (Flat01＝170 m², Flat02＝100 m²)   **Site Area** / 1400 m²

This building is located on a beautiful waterside plot, on the southern shore of the Lake Balaton. Its function is a summer cottage in which there are two separated flats. The larger flat is two-storey, the smaller one is on the second floor.

The most rooms are orientated to the lake. Neighbourhood of the shore and the effect of the height give almost the breath-taking feeling of floating over the water. Majority of the flat roof is covered with green roof. The outside façades are characterized mostly by white, dryvit plastering surfaces, large-panelled coverings, stone coverings of rustic effect and the varied rhythm of doors and windows. It was an expressed request of the owner to build in durable materials which could be resisting to the wet, extreme weather conditions with no maintenance even for decades.

For selecting the materials in addition to luxury and quality our aim was to realize a moderate style being in a close connection to the environment. For instance the Italian greyish green ashlaring like the colour of the stormy lake continues in the flats at several places optically connecting the natural environment to the indoor spaces.

The interior design of the house follows the modern exterior appearance. The natural materials used by the interior designer match well to the acrylic floor-covering, the large glass surfaces and the stainless and high-gloss materials.

This cottage has parameters close to passive houses so despite to its large basic area it can be economically operated. All the thick external thermal-insulations, the aerated panelled façade coverings, doors and windows of three-layer glazing, insulated shutters, the upper intensive green roof are for this aim.

Heating and cooling of the house, the consumer hot water and heating of the outdoor Jacuzzi are provided with soil sampling heat pump and the solar panel located on the roof. The various building equipments are harmonized by means of a computer building inspecting system. In shaping the final form of the house the owner having a good taste, the high-quality implementation and not at last the picturesque site had a great role. ●

Design Agency ·
Di Henshall Interior
Design

RIVERFRONT HOUSE

Location / Noosa Heads, Australia   Materials / Travertine, Jarrah and Black Ash Veneers, New Guinea Rosewood, Brushbox, Khaya Mahogany, Timber Strip Flooring, Natural Stone, Limestone, Antique Mirror, Gold Leaf Wallpaper

This waterfront home lacked warmth, drama and personality. The brief was to redesign the home with an Asian influence coupled with rich fabrics and colours that instantly make visitors feel at home. This was a change in design direction for interiors of houses in the locality where a neutral often white palette is generally the norm.

Design elements include selection of custom lights, design and manufacture of one off pieces of furniture and cabinetry and sourcing unique furniture pieces from Bali and around the world. Mixing a number of timber veneers creates interest and carries the eye from one area of the home to another.

Lighting was one of the most important elements of the interior design. To make the most of the void at the entrance of the house, a huge tear shaped pendant light in acrylic and balsa was installed to illuminate an antique carved timber panel on the wall. A spectacular translucent red custom made pendant light over the

dining table balances the strong reds in the sofa. A 'Blossom' pendant light with porcelain leaves in gold finish designed by Jeremy Cole has been fitted above the kitchen bench. Strip lighting under the stairs down to the living area give a warm ambience and the exterior butane glass lanterns are a feature.

Of particular interest is the custom designed and made wall entertainment unit in black ash textured veneer with veneered side panels and Jarrah veneer drawers. The TV is hidden behind pocket doors and includes a recess for the fire. Ebony flocked wallpaper with a diamond shaped pattern was selected to contrast with the black ash and hung on either side of the entertainment unit.

The kitchen was also custom desig ned and built, using New Guinea Rosewood with brushbox inserts. All wardrobes were refitted in Wenge or Khaya Mahogany colourboard.

After renovating and refurbishing this waterfront home, Di Henshall Interior Design was again engaged by the owner to create a gentleman's 'club room', as a separate space for entertaining guests.

To achieve a luxurious, warm and intimate atmosphere, Di used a combination of materials and textures, together with specialist lighting.

Narrow timber flooring with arrised edges in a dark grey walnut stain establishes a colonial feel, further enhanced by the large circular antique gold and walnut framed mirror over the fire. One entire wall is faced with hand selected rough hewn stone with a sandblasted hardwood timber sleeper set into the wall to form a mantel piece. The fire is set in a granite slab, with a smooth mocha crème limestone plinth below to provide contrast in colour and texture.

The custom designed bar includes a back lit feature front panel in Honey Onyx with benchtops in Titanium granite, and Ebony Macassar laminate to cupboards and drawers. Finishing touches include metallic gold leaf wallpaper and antiqued bronze mirrors behind the liquor shelves. The open cupboard above the bar has a powder coated grille illuminated by recessed Italian down lights.

Coconut wood feature panels surround the recessed wall mounted TV, illuminated by a series of pin lights to floor and ceiling. The ceiling itself is lined with antique mirrored panels.

Custom deep buttoned velvet sofas with black velvet armchairs are offset by a massive hand tufted wool floor rug in black and gold art silk. The custom made coffee table with onyx marble top has LED strip lighting to the underside, making it a focal point in the room. ●

CONTRIBUTORS

ARCO Arquitectura Contemporánea

ARCO Arquitectura Contemporánea (Contemporary Architecture) is an innovative company specialized in property development and interior architecture. The company experience in México and abroad is evident in the superior quality, transparency, personal and continuous service. The company considers that true architecture is developed based in the customer satisfaction, by the use of a language that shapes and expresses the intention in a aesthetic and functional result.

ARCO Arquitectura Contemporánea was founded by architects Bernardo Lew and José Lew which at the same time are in charge of the direction of the company. The main activities of the firm are: planning, architectonic project execution, interior design, consulting and coordination of structural projects, MEP systems, site direction, technical and economical management, coordination and construction supervision.

Bagnato Architects

Bagnato Architects was formed in 2007 by husband & wife team Dominic & Marie Bagnato after more than 15 years in previous practices. Both designers graduated from The University of Melbourne in 1992 with Marie embarking on a career with some well know Melbourne Architects and Dominic setting up private practice immediately.

The firm is dedicated to design excellence with a strong focus on client service. Based in cosmopolitan Carlton Victoria Australia, the practice has become renowned for inspiring architecture and interiors with a signature of luxury using natural materials & luxurious finishes.

With expertise in architecture, interior design & construction the practice has evolved to become known for its creative design solutions, stylish interiors & innovative planning, a signature style resonating in all their buildings.

Blanca Sanchez

Born in Paris to an American mother and Spanish father, Blanca came to England at the age six. She grew up in a 1930s house in Sunbury on Thames, Middlesex, accompanying her mother toantiques auctions as she (her mother) indulged her passion for antiques and individual pieces forthe family home.

Blanca trained at the Chelsea College of Art and Design, after getting an HonoursDegree from Durham University in Spanish with History, and after completing a postgraduatebusiness course at South Bank University.

Her interior design career started at Hill House Interiors in Weybridge, where she joined them in theirfirst week of business. After elevenyears with them she left to start her own award winning interior design company, Halo Design Interiors.

Halo has now worked on prestigious residential estates including the Crown Estate, Oxshott and The Wentworth Estate to name but two, with the value of the projects handled varying from around one million to over twenty million pounds.

Blu Water Studio

Blu Water Studio is an award winning design studio providing interior design consultancy services specializing in hotels, resorts and restaurants. Formed by highly talented designers, the team brings 20 years of experience in the design industry to create compelling and all-encompassing branded solutions.

The studio goal is to create unique and distinctive designs — strive s for passion and individualism at the core of each project, bringing the clientele instant recognition while maximizing the consumer's experience. The approach is to understand every aspect of our clients' brand and spirit, translating corporate identities into physical forms. By blending experience, innovation and solid business principles, Blu Water Studio creates memorable and inspiring experiences by architecting outstanding environments.

Craft Arquitectos

In 2008 the architect Alan Rahmane Azar, founded Craft Arquitectos, office focuses on the design, construction and marketing that aims to promote new perceptions and sensations hand spatial functioning, sustainable architecture, which is based on simple, clean lines.

They specialize in providing architectural solutions for different requirements: houses, apartments, offices, among others, as well as remodeling, expansion and construction to design, and interior design.

Craft Arquitectos to date has done many projects of a Residential, Commercial, Office, Landscape, Interior and several international competitions.

David Guerra Architecture and Interior

Founded in 2002 and located in Belo Horizonte, Minas Gerais, Brazil, the office David Guerra Architecture and Interior seek to combine creativity and functionality, always complying with the desire of the client in a singular and innovative way.

The Office acts in the architecture and interior design fields, and its works range from the small scale of the object, to the big scale of public and institutional buildings.

The team of architects and interns engage in extensive research to develop the projects, wherein the attention to the details and to the composition is always present.

Numerous projects of David Guerra Architecture and Interior have been awarded several times and have been published extensively, both in national and international media.

Dariel Studio

Dariel Studio is a multi-award winning interior design company founded in Shanghai in 2006 by French Designer Thomas Dariel. Since its establishment, Dariel Studio has completed over 60 projects of the highest quality in the main areas of design: hospitality, commercial and residential.

Dariel Studio manages to reach originality and creativity while also performing in project management, a double focus that led the company to be recognized and honored for its ability to lead projects from concept up to execution.

Dariel Studio's tailor-made approach focusing on clients needs has allowed the company to create a large portfolio of clients - private, entrepreneurs, luxury brands and big corporations - Chinese as International.

The studio counts today a team of 25 professionals coming from various countries and backgrounds driven by the same passion for design.

Di Henshall Interior Design

Established in 1988, Di Henshall Interior Design provides exceptional solutions for residential and commercial interiors, on time and on budget.

The design practice, based in Noosa, Queensland with a studio in Brisbane, covers all aspects of interior architecture, with work divided between design and consultancy, renovations and furnishings. This includes general space planning and building design, custom cabinetry design, selections of all internal fixtures and fittings, furnishings, window treatments — in fact, anything and everything that requires attention from an interior perspective.

Design Director Di Henshall is a UK qualified interior desi gner and registered builder. Having lived and practised in Australia since 1978, Di has embraced the lifestyle of the country, in particular the blend of inside and outside living so fundamental to the coastal cities and towns. She is able to translate this into designs and furnishings for homes and apartments that have an international appeal, yet still reflect their environment.

Di works with a team of fully qualified designers, strongly supported by administration and installation personnel.

On average, more than one hundred projects are completed every year across Australia in major capital cities including Sydney, Melb ourne and Adelaide, as well as in resort areas in North Queensland and on the northern and Central coasts of New South Wales.

Galeazzo Design

Know for joining together beauty and sustainability, Fábio Galeazzo work with timelessness. Creative in everything he proposes, he mixes materials with colors in a feisty and fearless way. Being know for a professional that don't repeats himself, his work has soul, where the past and the comtemporary live together in total harmony. He plays with the diachrony completely free and this is one of the trademarks of his language. Reread the time in the objects and the objects of time with his own style.

In 2004, founded Galeazzo Design, multidiciplinary company of architecture, interior design and product development, with a young and aligned team, being awarded nationally and internationally. His work is gaining prominence among the internacional press and it's been published in more than 50 countries.

Hartmann Designs

Hartmann Designs Ltd is an International Interior Design practice based in London committed to the creation of exceptional Design.

With a portfolio of work spanning Europe, Africa and the Middle East, the practice has worked on a wide range of projects including large-scale hospitality, corporate and high-end residential projects. All of the projects are individually developed with a strong emphasis on analysing and challenging the brief in order to meet the Client's specific aesthetic value, function and budgets.

As a result Hartmann Designs Ltd has developed a genuine understanding of its Client's requirements and delivered projects that are chic, timeless and above all extraordinary. Hartmann Designs provide quality of design and service through attention to detail ensuring a rare blend of practicality and charm.

Henrique Steyer

Henrique Steyer began his academic life studying advertising, and graduated as an architect in 2006. He is post-graduated in Advertising as an Specialist in Advertising Imagery and post-graduated in Strategic Design from POLI.design - Consorzio del Politecnico di Milano. In 2009 he attended the Trends Analysis Course in Milan, Italy. In 2010, he received the Young Talent Hunter Douglas Award, in Turkey, and once again in 2012. He writes columns about Design and Art on magazines and blogs. He lectured classes and workshops in Design graduation and post-graduation courses. His work has been published in more than 20 countries, including cover stories in important magazines around the world. Recently, he began creating artworks with modern themes and cosmopolitan appeal. De-sign furniture signed by him is being manufactured to cater to people looking for something innovative. His main feature is to distance himself from the conventional and propose something new, based on the assertion that "the trend is to follow no trends". His work has been compared to names such as Karim Rashid and Fabio Novembre.

Interior Marketing Group

Interior Marketing Group specializes in quickly transforming real state properties and average spaces into jaw-dropping luxury homes that even the most discriminating upscale Buyer will fall in love with.

Their exclusive warehouse of stunning furnishings, eclectic accessories, and original modern art, enable us to create the perfect balance of style, authenticity, and "WOW!" factor required to inspire bidding wars.

Founded in 2007 by real estate agent-turned-stager Cheryl Eisen, Interior Marketing Group has fast become NYC's leading luxury real estate staging & model home design firm. Drawing from her expertise in selling luxury real estate, Eisen's unique understanding of what drives Buyers' decisions to choose one property over another, inspired her to create a more strategic marketing-based approach to staging, which she called "interior marketing". This strategy has yielded an unprecedented 100% success rate.

Ippolito Fleitz Group

Ippolito Fleitz Group is a multidisciplinary, internationally operating design studio based in Stuttgart. Currently, Ippolito Fleitz Group presents itself as a creative unit of 37 designers, covering a wide field of design, from strategy to architecture, interiors, products, graphics and landscape architecture, each contributing specific skills to the alternating, project-oriented team formations. Our projects have won over 160 renowned international and national awards.

ITHAKA - Architecture and Design

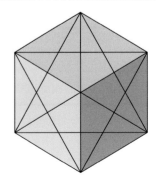

"ITHAKA - Architecture and Design" studio was founded in 1991. For more than 20 years, the studio completed over 100 projects.

Many completed projects, such as interior architecture of Moscow School of Management "SKOLKOVO" (interiors of the hotel, the hostel, the faculty club, the cottage community for professors and lecturers, deans house), Embassy of the Republic of Armenia to the Republic of Belarus, residence of the Ministry of Defense of RF in Krasnodar region, numerous private houses, apartments and mansions have turned into the hallmarks of the studio.

For the period from 1991 to 1999 the studio was mainly engaged in the restoration, construction and archaeological works in the Republic of Armenia. The studio has carried out various projects on the restoration and conservation of architectural monuments.

Since 2004 the company expanded the scope and field of its activities and was actively designing for private and commercial sectors, both in the Republic of Armenia and Russian Federation.

Kiko Salomão Arquitetura

Founded in 1995, the Office of Kiko Salomão Arquitetura has been since then developing projects for offices, homes, shops, restaurants and hotels and gained visibility via publication of its works in well known magazines such as Interior Design / U.S., Interni / Italy and Wallpaper.

Architect Kiko Salomão attended Business Administration and worked in the family concern until his call directed him towards studying architecture. In choosing a solo career, he was able to experience all the phases of a project as well as to apply his knowledge of administration in architecture. The natural consequence of this path was maturity, allowing him today to realize relevant project such as those for Bic Banco, Mattos Filho, Tiffany and several residential ones.

Entirely identified with contemporary, modernist and minimalistic influences, Kiko Salomão and his team imprint each job with their main characteristics: survey of new materials and a unique and refined detailing, providing an atmosphere of elegance together with sobriety of lines and cleanliness of information.

Representing a new generation, Kiko Salomão has already engraved his identity in the present architectural scenario. In conclusion, he is faithful to the most important quality of each creator: the contribution towards timeless designs.

Kurt Krueger Architect

Kurt Krueger Architect is a design centered architectural practice based in Los Angeles, California that specializes in design and construction. Our work responds to the specifics of its place while also satisfying our client's spatial and budgetary needs. We pride ourselves in the the craft of building and strive to create spaces that engage people while elevating a sense of interest to the individual qualities of each site and program. Every project contains a unique set of challenges, requiring a highly specific architecture that is at once functional and poetic. We value and aspire to create architecture that is graceful and timeless, concerned with space and light, context and place, texture and detail, and together enhances the overall experience.

Kurt Krueger, AIA, LEED AP was educated in the practice of architecture and design at Kansas State University. With an approach of learning by doing, he interned in Raleigh, North Carolina for Frank Harmon Architect and later worked for Rockhill and Associates in Lawrence, Kansas where he built several houses in Kansas City and Arkansas as a member of the construction crew. Using this training, he relocated to Los Angeles to work for the architecture firm Marmol Radziner & Associates, with a focus in design-build. After four years, he added to this experience by working another four years at ARYA Group, Inc, a high profile construction company in Los Angeles that specializes in design and construction. Kurt Krueger Architect was established in 2012 with a focus on design-build residential and commercial projects that are environmentally responsive and uniquely appropriate.

Lisa Garriss and Plum Design West

After graduating from Parsons School of Design in New York, Garriss found her niche in luxury hospitality design at Rockwell Group working on the landmark W Hotel New York. Following stints at Kohn Pedersen Fox Conway and Gensler in New York and Kerry Hill Architects and Wilson Associates in Singapore - where she had the opportunity to work with Giorgio Armani on Armani Hotels in Milan and Dubai - Garriss founded Plum Design (Singapore) in 2006, designing celebrated properties, including the Four Seasons Jimbaran Bay, the Padma Resort in Bali and the Alila Hotel in Goa, which won HICSA's coveted "Critic's Award" for Best New Hotel in India. Garriss opened Plum Design West, in Los Angeles, in 2009.

Plum Design and Plum Design West have provided interior design services for hospitality companies across the globe. From Singapore, Goa and Bali, to Los Angeles, Milan and Dubai, the visual story of each unique location is captured through Garriss' luxurious and dynamic interiors.

Completed projects include interiors for the Four Seasons Jimbaran Bay, the Padma Resort in Bali and the Alila Hotel in Goa, which garnered the "Critic's Award" for Best New Hotel in India by the HICSA Conference. In Los Angeles, Garriss recently completed five luxury residences in the exclusive Wilshire Boulevard high-rise Beverly West for Emaar Properties and is currently working with Warner Hospitality Group on their properties in New Mexico.

Lo Chen

Lo Chen specializes in high-end hospitality, residential, and commercial design. Currently, she is doing projects in US, Hong Kong, and Mainland China. Growing up in cosmopolitan Hong Kong, Lo studied Fine Arts in The Chinese University of Hong Kong and further pursued her study of Interior Design in Parsons School of Design. Lo has been with INTERIOR MARKETING GROUP since 2011 working in staging, model homes, and private residence projects. Two of IMG's projects (The Visionaire & 1212 Fifth) have been featured in ELITE Interior Magazine in Russia, both of which Lo was the Lead Designer.

Lucia Caballero

After school Lucia Caballero moved to Cape Town and studied Interior Architecture for 3 years at the Cape Peninsula University of Technology. After her studies she then made the big move to San Francisco, living with her sister, who is a fashion designer. Through a friend of hers Lucia Caballero secured an internship position for 4 months. Lucia Caballero learnt a lot in the short four months, all about American construction. SHE assisted on a penthouse apartment and a large house just a short drive from the Golden Gate Bridge. After the 4 months internship, SHE moved to London with her best friend to find work. Moving to Europe also gave me the opportunity to travel throughout Europe. She then secured a job at a small property development company based in Chelsea where she learned all about the London high end residential property market. She was the head interior designer there for five years and completed 9 projects of which one was an 18 000 sq. ft. house on Wentworth Estate.

Lucia Caballero then established Caballero in 2008 with her husband Hugh, who at that stage worked for himself as a property developer.

MSWW

MSWW - Ministerstwo Spraw We Wnetrzach (in easy translation – Ministry of Interior Affairs) is an interior design studio founded by Magdalena Konopka and Marcin Konopka. MSWW works mainly in the area of the Tri-City in Poland (Gdansk, Sopot, Gdynia). Nevertheless, also takes actions located away from our region – also abroad.

Marcin and Magda devote their energy and engagement into smuggling beauty to the space of everyday life. They look and listen. Propose, create. Fulfill needs. Their aim is to shape places where living, eating, working and leisure have their own, special and individual dimension. They see interiors as a mosaique of elements that try to arrange into a harmonious entirety. To gain proper effect MSWW deal with designing furniture, lighting, crafts as well as other activities that fit into the space or stay on the fringe of design.

The area of MSWW activities includes interior design seen from a wide perspective. They deal with private interiors (houses, apartments, suits etc.) and public interiors (offices, showrooms, restaurants, hotels, buildings of public use etc.)

Nasciturus Design

Nasciturus Design is a team of professionals, for whom arranging interiors is a real passion.

They constitute a team of professional architects, who, since 2004, have completed over 450 tailor made projects for Private and Business Customers. Their company's portfolio includes interior designs for flats and apartments, houses, hotels, restaurants, offices, doctor's surgeries and SPAs. Having established their own, unique style drawing inspiration from contemporary, classical, Retro & Art Deco, loft and avant-garde styles they managed to combine creative and functional architectural solutions, ideal proportions, care for the most minute detail as well as effective visual effects. Thanks to the variety of materials used on the projects, the interior spaces with a unique "personality".

Oliver Burns

Oliver Burns is an award-winning architectural interior design and development practice, committed to ethical standards in a luxury landscape. The company was established by Joe Burns and Sharon Lillywhite in 2004, with specialism in prime residential property, Oliver Burns has been responsible for the creation of more than 15 exquisite private homes in London and the south east of England over the last seven years. From opulent private homes to exclusive residential developments, Oliver Burns creates thoughtful, luxurious designs for discerning and influential clients.

Oliver Burns has embraced modern requirements by pioneering a bespoke, 360 degree property solution for clients. In addition to offering architectural interior design, Oliver Burns also has expertise in property sourcing, development appraisal, acquisition, planning, development management and marketing.

Oliver Burns has an ethical commitment to creating truly exquisite homes with the client's needs at the core of their work. The company is pioneering ethical alternatives in the luxury sector, not only implementing internal policies but also challenging suppliers to be more sustainable in business, either through dealings or product offerings. They are also working with local charity, Veterans Aid in the design and refurbishment of Belvedere House and are also Certified CarbonNeutral®. In addition, Oliver Burns has achieved Bronze level in the EcoStep awards.

Rolf Ockert Design

Prior to graduation from the highly regarded University in Stuttgart, Germany, Rolf spent extended periods of time gaining practical experience in renowned architectural practices in Germany and England. Amongst them Frei Otto, known for his design of tensile structures and research of natural structures and their application in building design, Michael Hopkins and Partners, best known for their redevelopment of Lord's in London and James Stirling, Pritzker Prize winning architect of iconic buildings such as the Staatsgalerie in Stuttgart and the Tate Gallery Turner Collection in London.

From 1997 to 2004 Rolf was Associate Director at Lippmann Associates, responsible for iconic projects such as the Andrew 'Boy' Charlton Pool in the Domain (RAIA Award 2003), the King George V Recreation Centre in the Rocks (RAIA Award 1999), the Butterfly House in Dover Heights and the MLC Aquatic Centre (RAIA Award 2004) as well as a number of other residential and public projects.

Rolf Ockert Design, commenced in 2004, has in a relatively short period of time created a rich portfolio of work, ranging from product design to residential, commercial and retail projects and masterplanning, located throughout Australia and also overseas, most recently in New Zealand, Japan and Switzerland. Many projects have been published in national publications as well as in books and magazines in, amongst others, Italy, China, Israel, the US and Russia with others in line to be published soon. Rolf is a member of the Australian Institute of Architects and the Board of Architects in NSW and Victoria.

SHH

SHH is an architects' practice and interior and branding design consultancy, formed in 1992 by its three principals: Chairman David Spence, Managing Director Graham Harris and Creative Director Neil Hogan. With a highly international workforce and portfolio, the company initially made its name in ultra-high-end residential schemes, where it both innovates and dominates, before extending its expertise to include leisure, workspace and retail schemes. SHH has won over 30 Awards for its projects, including Best Eco House (for its 'North London House with Green Credentials' project) and the 'International Interior Design' Award (for its Manchester Square office project) in 2010. SHH's work has appeared in leading design and lifestyle publications all over the world, including VOGUE and ELLE Decoration in the UK, Artravel and AMC in France, Frame in Holland, Monitor in Russia, DHD in Switzerland, ELLE Decoration in India, Habitat in South Africa, Contemporary Home Design in Australia, IDS in Malaysia and Architectural Digest in both France and Russia, with over 125 projects also published in 66 leading book titles worldwide.

Tamara Magel

Being in business for over 10 years, Tamara Magel has developed a reputation in design. Inspired by runway fashion, vintage looks and the contrast of masculine and feminine architecture and style. Tamara's aesthetic is unexpected, yet refreshing, bringing together curated looks from around the world.

Tamara Magel is the premier source of global-chic. Her experience in Interior Design with her signature home collection presents classic lines and balanced textures with an urban flair. A full service designer, Tamara sources all materials and customizes each project to meet the needs of the client creating a one-of-a-kind space embodying architecture and style.

Thomas Schoos

Artist, designer, developer and entrepreneur, Thomas Schoos is acclaimed as designer of some of the most successful hospitality venues in the U.S., ranging from Tao at the Venetian Hotel in Las Vegas, which has been the top-grossing restaurant in the U.S. every year since it opened in 2005, to Santa Monica's Huntley Hotel, which has won numerous awards and was featured in Architectural Digest. His design of Searsucker in San Diego contributed to it being voted by OpenTable the second most popular restaurant in the U.S. in 2011. In 2012, Morimoto Mexico City was named one of two finalists in the Hospitality Design Awards for Fine Dining. Schoos' success designing restaurants has led to ongoing partnerships with celebrity chefs like Masaharu Morimoto of Iron Chef and Brian Malarkey of The Taste, who rely on Schoos to create the evocative environments that will make their cuisine shine. The last few years have seen Schoos going more international, with projects in Beijing, Taipei, Thailand, London, the south of France and India. In addition to designing for clients, Schoos has recently been creating his own new restaurant brands, including a beach-themed coffee shop called Beach Nation and an Alpine restaurant called Ludwig Biergarten, both of which will open in L.A. later this year. Meanwhile, Schoos continues his career as an artist and painter, contributing original works to many of his projects.

Toth Project Architect Office

Toth Project's all members equally have intense professional calling in architecture. They area dynamic and youthful community based on strong friendship. All of them have progressive thinking and great ambition in desgin as a result of these they always bring to fruition their projects very efficiently. The most important for them give a hand to realize their client's dreams! Every new project is a personal challenge to their team, because they enjoy what they do.

They have been working for many years to connect the harmony of nature to living space. Their buildings are characterized by simple lines, natural and durable materilas. Toth Project prefers clear volumes, customised layouts, bright and spacious inner spaces. In the course of design procession they favour economical, feasible and sustainable solutions. Their office takes on complete architectural design, administration and consulting.

It is essential for them to find the common voice with their clients from the first moment of the design to the last build session. They believe that high quality depend on continous communication and close collaboration between every participant of design process. Toth Project follows the birth of the buildings, this is the key to successful projects. In their opinion a house is finished when the clients are completely glad and they could come in their gladness.

Whipple Russell Architects

Marc Whipple, the founder of Whipple Russell Architects, is the son of an American Diplomat, Marc Whipple grew up across Europe, Asia and Africa, whose rich cultures helped to shape his eclectic approach. Following his education at Eton College and London's prestigious Architectural Association School of Architecture, he became the protégé of internationally renowned architect George Vernon Russell. Russell, creator of show-stoppers like the Trocadero on Sunset Boulevard, the Flamingo in Las Vegas, as well as Samuel Goldwyn's home in Beverly Hills and the expansive University of California at Riverside campus, further broadened Marc's vision.

Twenty-five years ago, when Marc opened his own firm, he honored his late mentor by including his name in that of the practice. Since that time, Marc Whipple has demonstrated a range of scale and innovation that extends from intimate west coast life-style specific homes in the Hollywood Hills to the Sienna Hotel Spa Casino in Reno to a master plan for an island-spanning resort in the Caribbean. His firm, whipple russell architects, is noted for applying authentic materials, natural light and green technology to the marriage of elegant form and efficient function.

Whipple Russell architects, formerly known as The Russell Group Architects, has been featured in periodicals that include Metropolitan Home, Dwell Maga zine, Robb Report, the Los Angeles Business Journal, Home Beautiful, In Style Home, The Los Angeles Times and The New York Times.

Yunakov Architects

Yunakov – the group of designing companies founded and headed by an architect Sergiy Yunakov, the Laureate of the State award, Merit Architect of Ukraine, a corresponding member of the Ukrainian Academy of Architecture, an experienced teacher and architect for more than 30 years. 20-years architectural activity enabled the company to lead the architectural market of Ukraine.

Recently Yunakov presented the new direction - Home Design headed by Ivan Yunakov, which instantly became a successful and popular. The company creates and keeps archive of scientific and technical information. To develop project documentation we use present-day achievements and developments in the field of designing and engineering and in the field of IT- technology as well. Having strategic project for development and using techniques of project management in work the company has clear business-process structure, which ensures terms and performance standards required. We involve only highly-professional licensed companies for outsourcing, such as MEP-engineering. Architects and constructors of the studio improve their professional skills permanently by studying and assimilating the experience of domestic and foreign design companies. The field of activity of the company includes designing of residential, office, commercial, hotel complexes, administrative and industrial buildings, and cottage in Kiev and other cities of Ukraine as well.

ARTPOWER

Acknowledgements

We would like to thank all the designers and companies who made significant contributions to the compilation of this book. Without them, this project would not have been possible. We would also like to thank many others whose names did not appear on the credits, but made specific input and support for the project from beginning to end.

Future Editions

If you would like to contribute to the next edition of Artpower, please email us your details to: artpower@artpower.com.cn